ON
TOP OF THE
CLOUD

ON
TOP OF THE
CLOUD

How CIOs Leverage New Technologies to Drive Change and Build Value across the Enterprise

HUNTER MULLER

WILEY

John Wiley & Sons, Inc.

Published by John Wiley & Sons, Inc., Hoboken, New Jersey.
Published simultaneously in Canada.

No part of this publication may be reproduced, stored in a retrieval system, or
transmitted in any form or by any means, electronic, mechanical, photocopying,
recording, scanning, or otherwise, except as permitted under Section 107 or 108 of
the 1976 United States Copyright Act, without either the prior written permission
of the Publisher, or authorization through payment of the appropriate per-copy fee to
the Copyright Clearance Center, Inc., 222 Rosewood Drive, Danvers, MA 01923, (978)
750-8400, fax (978) 646-8600, or on the Web at www.copyright.com. Requests to
the Publisher for permission should be addressed to the Permissions Department,
John Wiley & Sons, Inc., 111 River Street, Hoboken, NJ 07030, (201) 748-6011,
fax (201) 748-6008, or online at http://www.wiley.com/go/permissions.

Limit of Liability/Disclaimer of Warranty: While the publisher and author have used
their best efforts in preparing this book, they make no representations or warranties
with respect to the accuracy or completeness of the contents of this book and
specifically disclaim any implied warranties of merchantability or fitness for a
particular purpose. No warranty may be created or extended by sales representatives
or written sales materials. The advice and strategies contained herein may not be
suitable for your situation. You should consult with a professional where
appropriate. Neither the publisher nor author shall be liable for any loss of profit or
any other commercial damages, including but not limited to special, incidental,
consequential, or other damages.

For general information on our other products and services or for technical support,
please contact our Customer Care Department within the United States at (800) 762-
2974, outside the United States at (317) 572-3993 or fax (317) 572-4002.

Wiley also publishes its books in a variety of electronic formats. Some content that
appears in print may not be available in electronic books. For more information
about Wiley products, visit our web site at www.wiley.com.

Library of Congress Cataloging-in-Publication Data:
Muller, Hunter
   On top of the cloud: how CIOS leverage new technologies to drive change and
build value across the enterprise/Hunter Muller.
      p. cm.
   Includes index.
   ISBN 978-1-118-06582-2 (hardback); ISBN 978-1-118-21443-5 (ebk);
ISBN 978-1-118-21454-1 (ebk); ISBN 978-1-118-21458-9 (ebk)
   1. Information technology—Management. 2. Technological innovations—
Management. 3. Cloud computing. 4. Chief information officers. I. Title.
   HD30.2.M8495 2012
   658'.0546782—dc23   2011038803

Printed in the United States of America

10 9 8 7 6 5 4 3 2 1

For Sandra, Chase, and Brice

CONTENTS

FOREWORD: THE FOUR HORSEMEN

I think it's safe to say that cloud computing is emerging from a period of chaos and entering an era of increasing standardization and stability.

That doesn't mean the cloud is fully mature, but it does appear to be heading in that general direction.

Why do I believe the cloud is evolving toward maturity? There are several reasons.

First, I believe that a dominant design for the cloud has already emerged. Almost every new technology undergoes a chaotic period of rapid development, followed by the emergence of a dominant design—a set of de facto standards.

For example, when the railways were initially constructed, there was little agreement on how wide apart to place the tracks. Each railway company had its own gauge, its own standards. Eventually, the companies settled on a single standard gauge.

Sometimes an innovative design is so powerful and so compelling that it becomes an icon of the new standard. The Model T Ford is a classic example. A more recent example is the iPod.

For the cloud, this phenomenon is represented by what I call "the four horsemen of dominant design." The four horsemen are:

1. Servers
2. Network
3. Storage
4. Software

The following table shows the dominant standards emerging in each of the four areas:

Servers	x86 architecture
Network	Internet (IP/TCIP)
Storage	Solid state (SSD)
Software	Software-as-a-Service (SaaS)

These "four horsemen" are the pillars of cloud infrastructure. They are also becoming the lingua franca of a new era in which the interplay between technology and the consumers of technology becomes much more focused on delivering value.

The emergence of a dominant design for cloud computing will likely enable a fundamental shift in information technology (IT) strategy. This shift will inevitably create challenges and opportunities.

Unlike most of our proprietary legacy systems, the cloud is a "tap into" technology. The "tap into" model is very different from the model we've grown accustomed to managing. As a result, IT leaders will be required to develop new skills and new capabilities. We will need to assume a more proactive leadership role in helping our companies make the most of the cloud's potential.

Throughout our history, FedEx has been focused on making connections, all over the world. It's the core of our business. That's one of the many reasons we find the cloud exciting—because it's a platform for making connections on a much larger scale than was imaginable in the past.

To me, the cloud represents the future. Here's a quick story illustrating why I feel this way: We were on a family vacation in the countryside. We had downloaded an app onto my digital tablet that enabled us to identify the stars in the night sky. Because the tablet has a cellular GPS, the app knows where I am. It can even tell which direction of the sky I'm pointing the tablet and the angle I'm holding it. Then it lights up a map of the sky, showing the stars and constellations. Naturally, my kids love it.

And while we're playing with the app and looking at the stars, I'm thinking, "All of the data resides somewhere else, and all of the calculations are being performed somewhere else. And I'm tapping into all that technology capability from the middle of a field."

The utility and potential of cloud computing seem virtually unlimited. Like emerging technologies of the past, the cloud is evolving from an early state of chaos into a state of greater maturity and stability. Now it's up to us, as leaders and executives, to devise practical strategies for leveraging the cloud's potential as a platform for innovation and success.

Robert B. (Rob) Carter
Executive Vice President of FedEx
Information Services and
Chief Information Officer of FedEx Corp.

PREFACE

What's *Really* New about the Cloud?

It seems to be a recurring phenomenon: I finish the manuscript for a book and I am ready to send it to my publisher. Then I find additional sources with fresh insights and great ideas. I call my editor, he growls at me, and we agree to extend the deadline so we can include the new material.

It happened with my first book, *The Transformational CIO*, and it happened with this book. Days before finalizing the manuscript, I was fortunate to secure interviews with three top thought leaders at IBM—Leslie Gordon, vice president, Office of the CIO, Application and Infrastructure Service Management; Jim Comfort, vice president, Integrated Delivery Platforms, Cloud Computing; and Lauren States, vice president, Enterprise Initiatives, Cloud Technology and Client Innovation, IBM Strategy.

Now my only problem was figuring out where to put their comments in the book. Fortunately, the solution to that problem became apparent almost immediately. The wisdom and insight that Leslie, Jim, and Lauren shared with me were so valuable that I knew they had to go right here, at the front of the book.

"Cloud puts power in the hands of the end user, and that can lead to a better financial equation for IT because of higher adoption rates and less under-utilization of resources. Cloud is changing the way we consume IT, and we're only at the beginning."

My conversations with these brilliant people covered a wide range of topics, but the main question I put to each of them was this: *What do you say to someone who tells you there's nothing new about the cloud?*

Here's a summary of their responses:

Leslie Gordon

Internally, we leverage cloud as an extension of existing strategy. From a technology perspective, it's not dramatically new. It's grounded in a lot of the same technologies that we already use. I see cloud as a natural turn of the crank. It's another abstraction of IT services, the next generation following virtualization and optimization of the infrastructure.

The cloud is not a one-size-fits-all solution, and it is not a panacea. You have to ask yourself, "Where does this approach fit in my organization? Where will it help me extend my strategy?" When you look at cloud from this perspective, it represents both an opportunity and a challenge.

One of the opportunities we identified early on was development and testing. We intentionally began in a low-risk area so we could really explore the potential of this new approach. It's proven to be a strong success. Now our developers can create and access test environments on demand, whenever they're ready, and wherever they are in the world—without engaging the test-build organization. We've taken the middleman out of the equation and enabled our developers to become more agile and productive.

We've also received tremendous positive feedback from our developers, and they've driven very high adoption of this new approach. The flexibility, speed, and freedom to do what they want really appeals to them.

We've also identified business analytics and storage virtualization as prime opportunities for using cloud, and we see strong potential in both areas. We've already used cloud to provide common BI services that can be applied to a large set of data warehouses. Taking that step has enabled us to analyze information more effectively, which is very valuable from a business perspective.

What's cool about cloud isn't the technology. What's really cool about cloud is how it changes the way people consume IT. Cloud puts power in the hands of the end user, and that can lead to a better financial equation for IT because of higher adoption rates and less underutilization of resources. Cloud is changing the way we consume IT, and we're only at the beginning.

Jim Comfort

The genuinely transformational aspect of the cloud is on the user side . . . the people who use IT. The cloud is about enabling developers to become five times more productive. It's about responding to market demand in hours or minutes, and not days, weeks, or months.

It's difficult for most CIOs to quantify those kinds of benefits. Most CIOs are great at quantifying what's going on in the IT shop. And that is the conundrum. The discussion rapidly becomes a very detailed conversation about nuts and bolts, speeds and feeds. CIOs are comfortable having these conversations. But when you talk about the cloud at that level, it's hard to see its value.

The fundamental abstraction of cloud is separating what from how. Separating what the user is trying to accomplish from how the underlying technology works.

Once you've made that separation, you can focus on the user. You can start asking, "What is the user's role? What is this user trying to do? What can we do in IT to make this user more productive?"

You aren't giving users infinite choice, you're giving users a range of choices that will help them become more productive. That's how you leverage cloud on the user side, by increasing labor productivity.

On the IT side, you leverage cloud by reducing costs and complexity. You build a service catalog that is efficiently constrained, standardized, and automated. Users get a range of choice that helps them become more productive, and IT gets lower costs and less complexity.

Now you are bridging two worlds, you are connecting IT and the business in a way that makes sense to both sides of the equation. That is the CIO's role during this transformational period: building bridges between IT and the other parts of the company. The cloud can help you build those bridges, which are essential to the company's long-term health.

> **"The fundamental abstraction of cloud is separating *what* from *how*. Separating *what* the user is trying to accomplish from how the underlying technology works."**

Lauren States

I think the prime focus should be on new business opportunities where the flexibility and speed-to-market advantages of the cloud delivery model can really bring value to the company.

We can argue about the technology itself all day long. Most of it is evolutionary. But I've seen it mature to the point where we can do things with it that we couldn't do before.

Virtualization is not an enabler for the business. The cloud, on the other hand, enables new business models. That's a big difference. It's not the technology that's revolutionary—what's revolutionary are the new ways we can apply the technology.

Where do you begin? Start by looking at your business processes, applications and workloads. Find out where it makes sense to move services into the cloud. And of course, you've got to consider data privacy, security, regulations, compliance, standards, tolerance for risk, governance, and all those requirements that are specific to your organization.

You'll have to negotiate with the cloud provider to make sure you get the service level agreements (SLAs) you'll need to deliver secure and reliable services to your end users, whether they are internal or external customers.

Some of the organizations we work with are moving into the cloud because of the economic benefits it can deliver in terms of reduced costs and added capabilities. Others see the cloud as a way to create new business services they can take to market and monetize. Those companies are saying, "With cloud, we can leverage our infrastructure and our technology to provide services to new customers and new markets."

In either case, you will need a new mix of skill sets in IT. Which skills will be important? Architecture, contract negotiation, governance, customer service, to name a few.

I recently saw a tweet listing the five stages of cloud adoption: denial, anger, bargaining, depression, and acceptance. I have it posted on my wall. It's funny, but it also reminds me that different people view the cloud differently. Most people are still in the earliest stages of adoption, and that's something you have to accept.

Personally, what I like best about the cloud is that I can carry it around in my handbag. The cloud delivers banking, shopping, reading, playing games, managing credit cards, talking to my family, communicating with work, building my professional network—all through mobile devices and all without me having to understand the many technologies behind it. That's really exciting.

I think this is driving toward a tipping point in IT, to a place where we can be much more productive and more flexible than ever before. I think this will be bigger than the transition from mainframes to client-servers, because this will enable us to do more—as companies, as consumers, and as a culture. For IT professionals, this opens up the possibilities of creating whole new sets of applications that are more collaborative, more data-intensive, more available, more networked, and much easier to use. Today, we're getting a glimpse of the future. We don't know how the story ends, but it's very exciting.

> **"Personally, what I like best about the cloud is that I can carry it around in my handbag. The cloud delivers banking, shopping, reading, playing games, managing credit cards, talking to my family, communicating with work, building my professional network—all through mobile devices and all without me having to understand the many technologies behind it."**

After my conversations with Leslie, Jim, and Lauren, I came away with a much stronger belief that the cloud is revolutionary in a business sense. The cloud will enable a new generation of business models—that seems perfectly clear. The fact that cloud computing is merely "evolutionary" from a pure technology perspective does not diminish its overall impact or lessen its potential as a transformational force. At the very least, it is another arrow in the CIO's quiver.

I was also deeply impressed by their shared insight about the cloud's impact on the role of the CIO. At minimum, the cloud's presence will require CIOs to develop new skill sets, whether or not they actually use cloud-based services. CIOs who do not acquire these new skills will likely find themselves at a competitive disadvantage as cloud services become more the new norm.

Leslie, Jim, and Lauren also mentioned a possibility that I hadn't previously considered, namely, the potential of cloud computing to serve as a template for managing an increasingly virtualized portfolio of IT capabilities. In other words, the cloud can become the model for the next generation of IT management. That, from my perspective, certainly makes the cloud worthy of deeper exploration.

As most of you already know, IBM is a major participant in the emerging cloud economy. IBM has publicly stated that the cloud is one of four key growth initiatives in its 2015 Roadmap. So far, the cloud has surpassed the company's expectations as a revenue engine. The company expects the cloud to play an important role in achieving its 2015 operating earnings per share (EPS) target of $20.

IBM's confidence in the ability of the cloud to deliver significant revenue isn't based on wishful thinking—as a cloud user, the company genuinely understands the value and the potential of the cloud as a fundamentally new model for enabling business transformation in rapidly changing markets.

In summary, what's new about the cloud isn't how it works, but what it enables us to achieve.

ACKNOWLEDGMENTS

The contents of this book are based primarily on the deep knowledge and wide experience that I acquired over nearly three decades as a consultant in the IT industry. But this book also represents several years of persistent research, involving dozens of interviews. I could not have completed *On Top of the Cloud* without leveraging the collective wisdom of many knowledgeable sources. I thank them sincerely for their time, their energy, their intelligence, and their support.

I am especially grateful to Rich Adduci, Ramón Baez, Becky Blalock, Mike Blake, Brian Bonner, Greg Buoncontri, Rob Carter, Trae Chancellor, Nicholas Colisto, Jim Comfort, Barbra Cooper, Tim Crawford, Martin Davis, Greg Fell, Matt French, Stephen Gold, Leslie Gordon, Allan Hackney, Kim Hammonds, Tyson Hartman, John Hill, Mark Hillman, Donagh Herlihy, Michael Hubbard, Randy Krotowski, Tony Leng, David Linthicum, Tod Nielsen, Bert Odinet, Tom Peck, Steve Phillips, Steve Phillpott, Mark Polansky, Tony Scott, Esat Sezer, Dave Smoley, Randy Spratt, Lauren States, Pat Toole, Clif Triplett, and Joe Weinman.

While researching and writing this book, I received invaluable assistance and ongoing support from my colleagues at HMG Strategy, Amanda Vlastas, Kristen Liu, Cathy Fell, and Melissa Marr.

I also extend my sincere thanks to Sheck Cho and Stacey Rivera, my editors at John Wiley & Sons, who had faith in the value of the project and were patient when I missed my deadlines. Kudos to Chris Gage and his production team for producing a book that is user-friendly and looks great.

I owe a special debt of gratitude to Mike Barlow, the co-author of *Partnering with the CIO* (Wiley, 2007) and *The Executive's Guide to Enterprise Social Media Strategy* (Wiley, 2011). Mike served as project manager for *On Top of the Cloud,* and his guidance was truly invaluable. In addition to being a talented writer and editor, Mike is a genuinely nice guy. Thank you, Mike!

Most of all, I want to thank my wife, Sandra, and our two sons, Chase and Brice, who put up with long nights of writing, endless phone calls, and lost weekends of heavy editing.

INTRODUCTION

Many of the great things in the history of our civiliza-
tion have been achieved by the independent will of
a determined soul. But the greatest opportunities
and boundless accomplishments of the Knowledge
Worker Age are reserved for those who master the art
of "we."

—Stephen R. Covey, from the foreword of the 2004
edition of *The 7 Habits of Highly Effective People*

About three years ago, I began writing about the convergence
of three major technology trends that I believed would radically transform the role of the modern CIO.

The trends were cloud, mobile, and social computing—in
that order.

Today, I would add advanced business analytics to the mix
of converging trends. And I might subtract the cloud.

Why remove the cloud? Well, I don't think it's fair to call the
cloud a trend any more. The word "trend" suggests a kind of
impermanence. Despite its vaporous name, cloud computing
has solid foundations. It is no longer mostly hype or fiction.
The cloud is real. It is a fact of life.

Gartner, the world's leading information technology (IT) research and advisory company, wrote in 2011 that "almost half of all CIOs expect to operate the majority of their applications and infrastructures via cloud technologies."

If we accept that cloud computing is here to stay, then it makes sense to get a firm grasp on what the cloud is and what it isn't.

> **"Almost half of all CIOs expect to operate the majority of their applications and infrastructures via cloud technologies."**

What it *isn't* is the end of IT. Why? Because the cloud is just another form of IT. As you know, IT technology tends to be additive. For example, when companies began using client-server technology, mainframes didn't suddenly vanish. The same thing happened when companies started buying PCs—they didn't throw away their client-server platforms. Some processes run better in mainframe environments, some processes run better in client-server environments, and some processes run better in desktop environments.

Part of the CIO's role is helping people figure out which technologies and which platforms do the best job of delivering the results that people need to achieve their business objectives.

Clearly, there are some parts of your IT portfolio that you will probably never put into the cloud. And there are some parts of your IT portfolio that you will happily send into the cloud.

So the big question isn't: *Will you or won't you use the cloud?* The big question is: *What will you use the cloud for?*

A New Business Model

Many of my friends and colleagues have expressed sincere skepticism over the cloud. Typically, they say the following:

"The cloud is not new technology."

"Most of the cloud is hype."

"The cloud will never provide the security we need."

To be fair, most of what they say is true—to a certain extent. Two foundational elements of the cloud—virtualization and networks—have been around for many years. So it's fair to say that a large chunk of cloud technology is not new.

I'm not really in a position to judge whether the cloud will live up to the hype surrounding it. Only time will tell. In today's media-rich culture, all new things are accompanied by irritating amounts of hype, and the cloud is no different. Suffice it to say that some of the hype is legitimate and some of it isn't.

Concern about the security of data in the cloud is mostly valid, but it assumes that the cloud in question is the public cloud and not a private cloud. We'll talk more about the differences among public, private, hybrid, and community clouds later on. For the moment, let's agree on two points. First, security *is* a relevant issue. Second, the type of cloud matters because some types offer more security than others. So making blanket statements about cloud security is like saying "I don't like laptops because of the security issues they pose."

Despite the uncertainty around the cloud, I am sure of one thing: The reason for learning about the cloud isn't because it represents a phenomenal new technology. The reason for learning about the cloud is because it represents a phenomenal new business model.

My instinct tells me that a lot of business leaders have already figured this out. And there lies the danger for the CIO: If you don't get on top of the cloud, the business will go around you and develop its own cloud strategy.

It's happened before, and it can happen again. Personally, I would prefer to see CIOs leading the charge.

"Thoughtfully Progressive"

My friend John Hill is not a wide-eyed optimist. He's smart, thorough, and rational. He is a former chief technology officer at Siemens, the global electronics and electrical engineering powerhouse.

> **"Most of us are inherently conservative and resistant to change. So we need to make a conscious effort to test the cloud, try it out, and find out where the benefits really are."**

When I asked him to describe the best way for CIOs to approach the cloud, he paused for a moment before saying, "Thoughtfully progressive."

Not surprisingly, John's take on the cloud is . . . thoughtful and progressive. Here's what he told me:

> *The cloud is similar to other parts of the IT landscape. The real issue isn't the availability of the technology. The real issue is the availability of skills and knowledge. For CIOs, that means doing pilot programs and allocating resources to evaluate the practical benefits of the cloud.*
>
> *Most of us are inherently conservative and resistant to change. So we need to make a conscious effort to test the cloud, try it out, and find out where the benefits really are. Now isn't the time to bet the farm; now is the time to build skills and knowledge.*

We'll hear more from John in subsequent chapters. He is one of many CIOs who generously shared their thoughts, insight, and wisdom with me as I wrote *On Top of the Cloud*. Essentially, this book is a collection of stories about smart, talented, and experienced CIOs who are trying to figure out the best ways to take advantage of the cloud and make it work for their organizations. I invite you to read their stories and learn from their experiences.

ON
TOP OF THE
CLOUD

Part I

Transformational Leadership

Chapter 1

The Rising Tide

Compared to the roles of other executives in the modern enterprise, the role of the chief information officer (CIO) has evolved quite dramatically over the past two decades.

In terms of status, the CIO has been elevated from a junior partner to a senior partner in the enterprise leadership circle. The CIO has a "seat at the table" and is considered a true member of the C-suite.

Status is often a matter of perception, however. What's *really* changed is the scope and breadth of the CIO's responsibilities. Let's turn the clock back 20 years. In those days, the CIO was the person responsible for keeping information technology (IT) systems running. The CIO's primary responsibility was making sure that IT did its job. Since a significant chunk of IT was devoted to maintaining back-office systems, the CIO was invisible to most of the enterprise.

The arrival of ERP (enterprise resource planning) systems removed some of that invisibility. Newer and more efficient ERP systems replaced older and less efficient legacy systems. There were disruptions and adjustments.

Nobody likes change, even when it's for a good reason. ERP put the CIO on the map. A major transformation was occurring, and the CIO was at the center of it.

While there is no question that ERP played a key part in elevating the role of the CIO as a corporate player, ERP was still a back-office function—which meant that it was invisible to most people in the organization.

The CIO as Rock Star

It took a unique convergence of several phenomena to permanently alter and elevate the role of the CIO. The phenomena included the development and successful marketing of inexpensive and relatively powerful personal computers; wide access to the Internet and the World Wide Web; and the rapid adoption of user-friendly Web browsers.

It didn't take long for visionary entrepreneurs and investors to connect the dots. Once it became apparent that an organization could conduct *real business* over the Internet, the role of the CIO suddenly became significantly more important. Information technology was seen as driving the next big wave of business. The CIO was the person who understood information technology.

Amid the excitement, the status of the CIO rose. But so did expectations. People now equated information technology with business success. They wanted the CIO to help them succeed. They wanted the CIO to help them make more money.

Let's pause and think about this for a moment. One day, you're the person responsible for keeping the IT systems running. The next day, you're one of the people responsible for making sure the company makes money.

This isn't a matter of doing a little extra work over the weekend. This is a monumental shift. There are huge differences between someone whose job is keeping the IT systems running and someone whose job is making money for the company. If you're the CIO of a large corporation or a publicly traded company, you are now in the spotlight. And being in the spotlight can get uncomfortable.

Real Stories from Real IT Leaders

In a very real sense, this book picks up where *The Transformational CIO* leaves off. One flows into the other. Even before I finished writing *The Transformational CIO*, I knew that I had to get this book started. They are two strands of a single thought, an unbroken narrative that examines the numerous challenges facing the modern CIO in a rapidly evolving global economy.

I certainly recommend that you read *The Transformational CIO*, but it's not required. You will learn a lot from this book. Like *The Transformational CIO*, it's constructed primarily from in-depth interviews with people who are probably very similar to you—executives, directors, and managers at companies where IT is expected to perform the increasingly complex dual role of maintaining day-to-day operations *and* providing strategic advantages in highly competitive markets.

Learning from Listening

I spend practically all day listening to CIOs. It's the central and most important part of my role as president and chief executive at HMG Strategy, the leading producer of CIO thought leadership events in North America. The success of my business depends largely on my ability to have meaningful, valuable conversations with senior IT leaders at companies all over the world.

Essentially, my workday is a continuing series of conversations with CIOs. I mostly listen, because it's the best way to learn. I've filled notebooks with snippets from these conversations, and several years ago I decided to use some of them as the foundation for a book. The notebooks gradually evolved into my first book, *The Transformational CIO*. The book's success led to a second book, which you are reading now.

What makes these books different from other IT management books is that they are not dry products of academic research and/or thinly disguised promotions for narrow viewpoints about specific kinds of software.

The Transformational CIO and *On Top of the Cloud* are unbiased and minimally edited words spoken by the leaders and executives who make critical decisions about the advanced technologies that enable the modern enterprise.

Like *The Transformational CIO*, this book is a collection of stories, anecdotes and insight, knowledge and wisdom that I've collected from hundreds of conversations. *On Top of the Cloud* is pure reality, distilled into a highly readable format. These are the voices of your peers, sharing their real-life stories.

More Than Technology

Although there's a lot about the cloud in this book, this is not a book about the cloud, per se. This is a book about leadership. It's filled with stories about leaders who have leveraged the power of newer technologies to grow revenues and improve profits. In short, they are business executives first and technology executives second.

Today's successful CIOs are true executive leaders. They are educated, experienced, and corporate-savvy—in a meeting, there's no way to tell them apart from their C-level peers. Modern CIOs know how to work collaboratively at the highest levels of the organization. They *have* a seat at the table, they feel comfortable in the executive boardroom, and they know what's expected of them.

The Real Challenge Is Organizational

Tod Nielsen is co-president of Applications Platform at VMware, the global leader in virtualization technology. When I asked Tod to list the major challenges facing organizations as they move toward greater use of the cloud, his reply focused on people and processes—and not on technology. Here's a summary of what he told me:

It's easy to talk about the technology and the architecture of cloud services. They are definitely significant pieces of the conversation. But the real issues that we are seeing have more to do with change management, education, building trust, and transforming the organization.

For example, the classic IT org chart is a hub and spoke model in which database administrators, systems administrators, and network administrators are all separated. But you can't have those separate and distinct silos in a cloud or virtualized computing model.

In the cloud, all of those IT functions are interdependent and have to work together. So it is a real issue setting up the right organizational structure. A lot of folks don't think about the cloud from an organizational perspective. As a result, they get to a certain point and they hit a brick wall.

The question you really need to ask is, "How do we pivot the IT organization so it can accomplish something that's never been done before?"

We see some IT organizations experimenting with best-practice teams. They don't change the formal org structure of IT, but they create these active entities that, over time, become permanent fixtures. These best practice teams essentially pilot the transformation. They can help break down the walls between silos. And they can also attract funding, because they are often driving changes that can result in cost savings.

"The question you really need to ask is, 'How do we pivot the IT organization so it can accomplish something that's never been done before?'"

I asked Tod to describe the typical composition of a best-practice team. Here's what he recommends:

First and foremost, you need someone who is a die-hard believer and an evangelist. You need to anoint a champion. Every organization has someone like that. You just need to find that person. Your champion can come from any of the silos. You'll have to look around. Just make sure that you pick someone with the passion to drive a real transformation.

You want your best-practice team to have a strong proportion of cloud believers, but you also want to include some naysayers. They will give the team credibility, and they are the ones you will need to win over early on.

Remember, there are two kinds of IT people: classic IT and what I call the "raw developer community." The developers tend to be active, dynamic, and always ready to try something new. They want to have a dialogue, and they're often ahead of the vendors.

Classic IT people, on the other hand, are a more varied group. Many of them realize that a new wave is coming, and they want to get on top of it. And some are very resistant to change.

I was chatting a few months ago with a CIO who told me that no one in his organization is permitted to use the public cloud. I asked him how many people in the company have iPads. He conceded that a "fair number" of people in the company have iPads. I said, "I guarantee you that your iPad users have Dropbox accounts, and therefore you have corporate documents in the public cloud." He said, "No way, that can't be true." A week later, he called me and said, "Wow, you were right. They're using the public cloud, even though we told them not to."

"First and foremost, you need someone who is a die-hard believer and an evangelist. You need to anoint a champion. Every organization has someone like that. You just need to find that person. Your champion can come from any of the silos. You'll have to look around. Just make sure that you pick someone with the passion to drive a real transformation."

Tod makes an excellent point with this anecdote. Chances are that your IT organization includes a truly diverse range of opinions and beliefs about the cloud. Part of your role as CIO is making sure that everyone—whether they love the cloud or hate it—is brought up to speed and understands what the cloud can and cannot do. Only then can you have an informed debate over the cloud's merits.

Leadership Is Essential

Meet Randy Krotowski, CIO Global Upstream at Chevron. It's hard not to like Randy. He's one of those naturally open and optimistic people—he's a good guy and a brilliant executive.

Randy leads an organization of about 2,500 people spread across 23 countries. Whenever you're managing an organization of that size, there will be challenges to resolve. In his formative years as a chemical engineer, and later on in a variety of leadership roles at Chevron, he learned that in many situations, there's no substitute for hands-on experience and face-to-face meetings. So he tends to travel a lot. On one recent trip, he logged 129 travel hours in 14 days.

"I went out and I talked to the people I had to talk to. It's part of the job," says Randy. "You're only as good as the leadership and the talent you have within your organization. If you can get 2,500 people moving in the same direction, you can do some amazing things."

Randy speaks with the calm and friendly demeanor of a true leader. In many ways, he seems like a role model for the modern transformational CIO.

> **"You're only as good as the leadership and the talent you have within your organization. If you can get 2,500 people moving in the same direction, you can do some amazing things."**

"I got some great advice a long time ago: Be an enterprise leader first, and a technology leader second," says Randy. "As an enterprise leader, my job is helping the company figure out what it needs and where it needs to go to be successful in the long term. How do we respond to the changes going on in the world around us? How do we make sure that we're focusing our attention on the things that really matter? Those are the big questions I'm dealing with."

Of course, he is still responsible for making sure that IT executes its mission. "The CIO is hired to have a point of view and a strategy. But if IT doesn't execute, then your point of view and your strategy won't matter."

Nevertheless, Randy describes himself as "more of a strategist than an operational leader." That doesn't mean that he isn't versed in the technology—it just means that he knows his role is providing leadership, not technical expertise.

> *There are plenty of people here who know more about IT than I know, and that's fine. In a large organization, you can only focus on a few things at a time. If you focus too closely on the details, then you might wind up going around in circles, and your perspective will be limited to the short-term. But if you're trying to have an impact on the direction of the enterprise, you need a point of view that stretches at least five to ten years into the future.*

I truly believe that Randy has defined the critical difference between the traditional CIO, whose primary role was keeping the lights on, and the transformational CIO, whose primary role is helping the senior executive team guide the enterprise. "You're brought in as CIO because they want you to succeed. Everyone is betting on you," he says.

But if you don't deliver, your credibility can vanish—so a big part of the CIO's job is maintaining his or her credibility. Randy says,

> *Credibility is the currency you have in the organization. If you have tons of credibility, you can do big things. If you don't, then you're going to be running servers and data centers, because that's all they'll trust you with. Credibility is built by*

making and keeping commitments. And when you can't keep a commitment, you have to be transparent and explain why. You have to come clean. A lot of people can't do that—they'd rather not surface a problem and try instead to fix it by themselves. But realistically, if you don't surface a problem, people won't pay attention, and you aren't going to get the help you need to fix it.

> **"Credibility is the currency you have in the organization. If you have tons of credibility, you can do big things."**

For the transformational CIO, transparency is a fundamental building block of superior execution and credibility. Both are necessary to maintain the trust and confidence of senior management.

Chapter 2

IT Does Matter

Back in 2003, Nicholas Carr wrote an article for the *Harvard Business Review* entitled "IT Doesn't Matter." The article is now legendary—several CIOs referred to it during our conversations—and it still incites vigorous debate. As most of you already know, Carr argued that IT would become a commodity, like electricity, that provides basic capabilities, but not strategic advantages.

Carr's article sparked some furious debate. Many people thought he was right. Some even said that the arrival of cloud computing was the final nail in IT's coffin. Once everything moved to the cloud, they reasoned, there would be little need for a robust corporate IT function. The CIO would be relegated to the role of custodian or supervisor—the person who called the cloud vendor in the unlikely event that something went wrong.

Caught up in the hype, writers and analysts saw the cloud as living proof that Carr's vision of the future was both sensible and accurate. Of course, it didn't quite work out that way.

The responsibilities of the CIO, the burdens on IT, and the expectations that technology must deliver real business value have dramatically *increased*, not diminished, since Carr's famous article was published.

So at the risk of stating the obvious, it's important to filter out the hype and stay focused on what we know is real: IT *does* matter, and the CIO is expected to lead IT in such a way that it delivers value to the enterprise. Moreover, the CIO is expected to provide leadership across the entire enterprise. In other words, now that the CIO has a seat at the C-level executive table, the CIO is expected to provide C-level executive leadership.

Stay Focused on Delivering Value

Over the course of writing and researching this book, I have conducted more than 70 interviews with CIOs and IT industry leaders. Time and time again, they told me this: The cloud is not *the* solution. The cloud is *part* of a solution, one piece of a much larger puzzle.

There is no question that for many organizations, software-as-a-service (SaaS) makes sense today. And I think it's reasonable to say that in the near future, the business benefits of platform-as-a-service (PaaS) and infrastructure-as-a-service (IaaS) will become increasingly clear. We're on a path, but we're not there yet.

Here's something we can say with certainty: For the vast majority of businesses and organizations, the cloud represents an evolutionary step away from the traditional IT paradigm and a step toward something new.

Let's take a moment to discuss the difference between a "step" and a "leap." A leap is okay if you know where you're leaping from and where you're leaping to. If you're not sure, don't leap.

Sometimes the smart strategy is taking several exploratory steps. At this particular moment in history, it's important for CIOs to be conducting pilots and experiments with cloud-based offerings. That's really the only way for the CIO to discover what the cloud can and cannot provide. There's no substitute for first-hand knowledge, so now's the time to put some skin in the game and find out what the cloud can do.

At the same time, the CIO must remain focused on the much more difficult task of leveraging technology to create business growth and value. That's what the CEO and the stakeholders want—*business growth and value*. No matter what they might say, they really aren't interested in the technology itself. On the other hand, they *do* care very much about results you can help them achieve.

The cloud is a means to an end, not the end itself. There is some very cool technology in the cloud. But today's CIO is expected to deliver more than cool technology—the CIO is expected to deliver measurable business value.

So now the real question becomes:

How does the CIO deliver real value?

If that is the primary question, the logical follow-up question is:

Should the CIO focus on achieving increased operational efficiency or continuous innovation?

And the next logical follow-up question is:

Can the CIO achieve both?

Replacing the Perpetual Pendulum

Randy Spratt is the EVP, CIO, and CTO of McKesson Corporation, one of the world's leading health care services and information technology companies. McKesson is currently ranked 14th on the Fortune 500. But even if McKesson were smaller and less prestigious, it would be worth knowing more about, since its primary business is helping hospitals, physicians, and pharmacies deliver high-quality health care by reducing costs, streamlining processes, and improving the quality and safety of patient care. What McKesson does has an impact on all of us and our families.

Randy was a keynote speaker at our CIO Executive Leadership Summit in San Francisco last year, and I very much wanted to include an interview with him in this book.

When chatting about the challenges confronting CIOs, Randy uses a great image: a "perpetual pendulum" in which the CIO's priorities swing back and forth between the perceived needs of the business and the perceived needs of IT. The business seeks speed and agility to generate top-line growth; IT seeks efficiency and security to improve the bottom line. Depending on the state of the economy and the overall health of the business, executive management will swing from one extreme to the other—and woe to the CIO who doesn't follow the swinging pendulum.

Now imagine replacing the "perpetual pendulum" with a virtuous cycle in which IT is constantly evolving through phases of innovation, adoption, standardization, and commoditization. Instead of a wasteful battle between proponents of top-line and bottom-line growth strategies, you have a smooth and continuous evolution that enables both strategies to coexist and to support each other constructively.

Let's look at the virtuous cycle in greater detail. The innovation phase covers the development of new products and new services. Clearly this is about top-line growth. The adoption phase is all about customer satisfaction and customer experience. This phase is also focused on top-line growth. The accompanying graphics from Randy illustrate this concept.

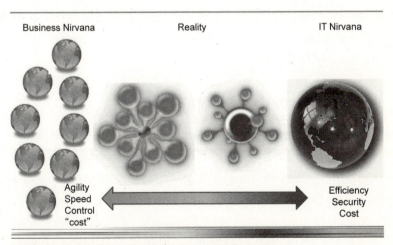

Business Nirvana   Reality   IT Nirvana

Agility
Speed
Control
"cost"

Efficiency
Security
Cost

IT Life Cycles in Value Creation: *Perpetual Pendulum*

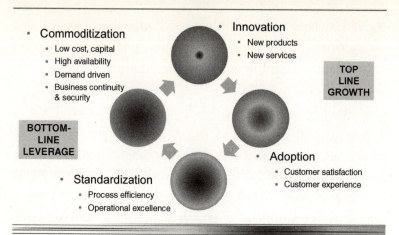

- **Commoditization**
  - Low cost, capital
  - High availability
  - Demand driven
  - Business continuity & security

- **Innovation**
  - New products
  - New services

TOP LINE GROWTH

BOTTOM-LINE LEVERAGE

- **Adoption**
  - Customer satisfaction
  - Customer experience

- **Standardization**
  - Process efficiency
  - Operational excellence

IT Life Cycles—Another Version: *Virtuous Cycle*

Remember, the cycle is constantly evolving toward greater maturity, so the next two phases—standardization (process efficiency, operational excellence) and commoditization (high availability, demand-driven, business continuity, security, low cost)—will be all about bottom-line leverage.

In the virtuous cycle described by Randy, the goals of IT and the goals of the business aren't mutually exclusive—they are complementary and supportive.

Driving the Innovation Agenda

Tom Peck is the CIO of Levi Strauss & Co. A graduate of the U.S. Naval Academy and the Naval Postgraduate School, Tom began his career in the U.S. Marine Corps, where he held a variety of finance and technology jobs.

When I asked him to describe the major challenges facing modern CIOs, the item at the top of his list was "driving an innovation agenda." Here's how he describes that agenda, in his own words:

> *Levi Strauss & Co. is a 150-plus-year-old company that has been innovating since 1873, the year we created the world's first blue jeans. Throughout our long history we've inspired change in the marketplace, the workplace, and the world. But bringing innovation through technology and ultimately to the way we sell and how we interact with consumers is new to us.*
>
> *We've all discussed and read about the importance of CIOs and IT leaders being influential and "having a seat at the table." Nowhere is this more true than in driving the innovation agenda. It's easy to chase too many or too few ideas. It's sometimes difficult to find seed money for innovation. And oftentimes the business doesn't know what they want or what IT may be capable of delivering. One of my favorite quotes is from Henry Ford: "If I had asked people what they wanted, they would have said faster horses."*
>
> *. . . we must stay at a reasonable pace with the overall trends in the consumer marketplace and "@ home" technologies. I truly believe that individual people (end users and our employees), not IT organizations, will fuel the next wave of technology innovation and adoption. Thus it's important we stay relevant, innovative, creative, and closely aligned with the workforce we are trying to enable.*

> **"I truly believe that individual people (end users and our employees), not IT organizations, will fuel the next wave of technology innovation and adoption. Thus it's important we stay relevant, innovative, creative, and closely aligned with the workforce we are trying to enable."**

Driving innovation means keeping close tabs on the trends and patterns of global markets. One of the most powerful—and perhaps least anticipated—trends is the consumerization of information technology. Here are Tom's thoughts on the topic:

The reality is that many of us have powerful computer systems at home, and social computing tools like Facebook, Twitter, blogs, etc., are a part of our everyday lives. As technology plays an increasingly important role in our personal lives and we become accustomed to the power, convenience, flexibility, and connectedness of consumer technology experiences, we want those same capabilities to help us at work.

However, in most cases we aren't being given the tools. It wasn't that long ago that we learned about and experienced cutting-edge technology in the workplace. How quickly that has changed—as consumers, we now have access to and take advantage of the latest technology to hit the shelves or even be streamed as a service through our high-speed broadband connections.

The reality is that corporate IT, for the most part, lags in adoption and deployment cycles. . . . We often align to bring business the "latest" offerings for the enterprise . . . only months or even years late. It's further complicated by the new influence of the millennial generation.

CIOs cannot always say "no." We need to adopt and embrace consumer technologies, learn from our users (who are also consumers), and put the appropriate guard-rails in place to allow for agility without sacrificing security, total cost of ownership, and support levels.

> "CIOs cannot always say 'no.' We need to adopt and embrace consumer technologies, learn from our users (who are also consumers), and put the appropriate guardrails in place to allow for agility without sacrificing security, total cost of ownership, and support levels."

Driving continuous innovation requires a different approach to managing IT. Tom's thoughts on managing the new IT "ecosystem" are especially relevant:

The days of doing business with one company for hardware, another for software, etc., are gone. Today, the modern CIO is almost more like a supply chain officer—a supply chain of technology offerings—managing an ecosystem of partners, suppliers, devices, in or out of the cloud, and more. No longer do you do a deal with one partner in the room.

Today's ecosystem is becoming more and more complex. Even the most experienced CIOs can get confused. We are seeing the perfect storm. Tech spending is favorable. There is a favorable cycle for product renewals.

Consumers continue to become more "tech friendly." We are watching device convergence and lower-priced, more capable computing chips. Mobility and cloud offerings further complicate the ecosystem as your friendly supplier now offers to do "everything" for you.

This is leading to what I call "vertical integration"—where companies lack a solution, they're acquiring or forming strategic partnerships. It started years ago when hardware and software companies started acquiring services businesses. Now you're seeing integration between hardware and software, on-premise and cloud, mobile and not, and much more.

It begs the questions of what will happen to niche players who lack the "verticalness." A handful of cash-rich companies are consolidating power . . . expanding into new business or product lines . . . possibly making it harder for small or mid-size competitors to break through. The largest tech companies (like Apple, Oracle, Google, Microsoft, and others) generated nearly $70 billion in new cash between 2007–2009 compared to nearly $14 billion for the other 65 tech companies in the S&P 500 index. From the end of 2007 to end of 2009, the 10 richest tech companies increased their cash levels by 48 percent to $210 billion.

The gap is at an all-time record high. This imbalance is changing how businesses behave. CIOs must figure out not only whom to negotiate and source with, but how to leverage the capabilities across multiple service providers in the global marketplace.

We will hear more from Tom in Part II of this book when we look more closely at leveraging the cloud to drive value for the enterprise.

> **"CIOs must figure out not only whom to negotiate and source with, but how to leverage the capabilities across multiple service providers in the global marketplace."**

It's All a Question of Perspective

Mark Hillman is VP, Strategy and Product Line Management at Compuware Corporation. Compuware provides software, experts, and best practices to ensure that technology works

well and delivers value. The company serves 7,100 customer organizations worldwide, including 46 of the top
50 Fortune 500 companies and 12 of the top 20 most visited
U.S. Web sites.

Basically, you hire Compuware to make certain that your
technology is performing optimally. And if your technology
isn't delivering the appropriate level of value, Compuware
will help you figure out how to improve its performance.

Our conversation ranged far and wide, but one of Mark's
observations about cloud computing really struck home. We
were talking about all the usual concerns around the cloud.
Security, of course, topped the list. But here's what Mark said
that pushed the conversation into high gear:

"Security is critical, but you should look at it as an item on
your due-diligence checklist, not as a barrier."

In other words, you manage security in the same way that
you manage all the other challenges that you encounter in
your role as an IT leader.

> **"Security is critical, but you should look at it as an
> item on your due-diligence checklist, not as a barrier."**

Mark's comment about the due-diligence checklist got me
thinking about how different kinds of CIOs sometimes look
at the world from very different perspectives.

For example, traditional CIOs generally see themselves as *risk-averse*, while transformational CIOs are more likely to see themselves as *risk-aware*. Another quick example: Where the traditional CIO might focus on *service levels*, the transformational CIO is more likely to focus on *business continuity*.

I put together a little table showing some of the differences between "traditional" and "transformational" approaches to IT leadership. I hope it engages your interest and sparks some debate.

"Traditional" worries mostly about . . .	"Transformational" also focuses on . . .
Security	Speed to market
Cost reduction	Business continuity
Service levels	Customer satisfaction
Minimizing risk	Managing risk
Process	Results

In real life, the two perspectives aren't separated by a brick wall. They represent subsets of your larger responsibility as an IT leader to drive change and innovation across the enterprise.

Chapter 3

The Engine of Innovation

We talk a lot these days about the need for continuous innovation. But who is more responsible for innovation, IT or the business?

"It's a balancing act," says Rich Adduci, senior vice president and chief information officer at Boston Scientific. "We certainly want guidance from the business. Under our governance model, it's up to the business to sort out where we make our investments. At the same time, we can't allow every project requested to go forward. If we're going to continue being efficient and effective, we need to get the most value from the solutions we deliver. Sometimes we have already invested in a solution, and we need to leverage that investment."

Rich makes a great point. As IT leaders, we need to be innovative. But we also need to know how to say no—tactfully, gracefully, and respectfully—when the business requests a solution that duplicates an existing capability, appeals to a limited number of users, or creates more problems than it solves.

"There has to be a business case for making the investment, or you're doing the shareholders a disservice," says Rich. "That's why you need good governance and strong leadership, so you can concentrate on adding value to the company. You cannot afford to waste money."

The consumerization of technology has been great for consumers, but it can make headaches for the CIO, especially when the business asks for devices or solutions that cannot be integrated smoothly into existing infrastructures.

"There will always be that bright shiny object that attracts attention, a niche solution that people like better than what they have today," says Rich. "But if everyone acts independently, then nothing connects—and you have a big mess. The hard part of IT is getting everything to work together so information flows seamlessly across a tapestry of different platforms and solutions. That isn't easy, but it's an important part of the job."

> **"The hard part of IT is getting everything to work together so information flows seamlessly across a tapestry of different platforms and solutions."**

Rich recently launched an innovation incubator within IT to provide seed money for internally developed projects that show promise. "We can take an idea to the proof-of-concept stage, offer a live demo, and show people the opportunity," says Rich. It's a "fail fast" approach to innovation that keeps the creative juices flowing without wasting precious resources.

In some instances, it makes sense for IT to take the lead in mainstreaming new technology. For example, the IT group at Boston Scientific recently rolled out an initiative to equip the sales force with tablets. Rich says that when he introduced the idea to the members of his leadership team, some raised concerns about security, connectivity, integration, and other potential problems.

"There were a thousand reasons not to do it. But part of our mission in IT is bringing innovation to the business. I remember pointing to the tablet and saying, 'This is clearly the right answer, so let's go do it.' And we did, and it was a home run."

Were there some risks involved? Yes, but Rich and his team identified the risks and figured out how to manage them. "You cannot be innovative without taking some risks. If you think you can mitigate all the risks and still be innovative, you're wrong. You have to be willing to jump a little, to make a leap. If you're not willing to do that, you cannot aspire to be innovative."

I think that's a wonderful way of framing the challenge of bringing true innovation to the enterprise. You need strong governance, strong leadership, and strong relationships. And you need a certain amount of courage—because you can't predict the future with total certainty. There will always be risks. Transformational CIOs understand the risks, weigh them judiciously, and then make decisions that will add value to the enterprise.

Bringing Innovation to the Surface

Rich's story started me thinking about the role of the CIO as a champion of innovation. Obviously, the CIO can't be held personally responsible for innovation. But the CIO can certainly help create an environment and a culture that encourages and supports innovation across the enterprise, no matter where it arises.

Innovation comes in many forms and dimensions. You can find innovation in every part of the enterprise: procurement, HR, finance, IT, operations, organizational development, product development, manufacturing, sales, marketing, distribution, fulfillment, customer service. Human beings are born to innovate. It's part of our DNA.

Because innovation can lead to competitive advantages in business, it is considered the key to growth and success. That's why we spend lots of time thinking, talking, and writing about it.

Despite the overwhelming importance of innovation, we often find it difficult to create work environments that are truly receptive to innovation. Sometimes, in our haste to streamline business processes and reduce inefficiency, we act as though innovation were an enemy instead of our friend. The resistance to innovation is understandable, because innovation brings change, and nobody likes change.

So when I heard this story from Allan Hackney, SVP and CIO at John Hancock, I knew I had to share it with you. The story begins in June 2010. Like many companies, John Hancock was recovering from the impact of the global recession. Many of the company's employees were worried about the future. Management was looking for ways to boost morale and reignite the spirit of creativity that had led the company to success in the past. Here's the rest of the story in Allan's own words:

> *We decided to hold a contest. The challenge was to develop a practical way for managing mobile tablets, which had been recently introduced in the marketplace. You had 90 days to develop a prototype, using a mobile tablet provided by the company. You would have to demonstrate your prototype to the rest of the company at a special event. Your prototype would be judged by a panel, and if you won, you would keep the tablet. It was that simple.*

> *We called the contest Project Launchpad. It was open to all employees in the U.S. and Canada—about 7,000 people. We estimated that maybe 25 to 40 ideas would be submitted. We received 176 ideas—more than four times the maximum amount we had anticipated. We had ideas submitted from every level and every part of the organization, everyone from nonexempt hourly workers to executive vice presidents. It was truly amazing. People were coming out of the woodwork with great ideas.*

> *We had formed a cross-functional team of five employees to manage the contest. They went through every idea submitted and winnowed the field down to 26 employees working on 14 projects (similar ideas were folded into one project to avoid duplication).*

> *At the end of the 90 days, the contestants demonstrated their projects at our two main sites in Boston. The team*

leading the contest had picked four senior executives to judge the demos. Some of the judges were selected because they were skeptical about mobile computing, and we wanted them to experience working with mobile tablets. We even built a little tablet app for scoring the projects.

The judges loved it. They awarded prizes for first, second, and third place. Best of all, we adopted all three of the winning projects and put them into production. One of the employees who entered the contest—someone from our retirement planning business—was reassigned to work full-time on developing his idea. And he's not an IT guy!

The real lesson we learned is that there is a huge amount of talent and creativity within our organization. We also learned that no single department has a lock on innovation. The contest enabled us to tap into the knowledge and creativity of our employee base. Our people have great ideas, and we gave them the opportunity and the resources to show what they can do.

> **"The real lesson we learned is that there is a huge amount of talent and creativity within our organization. We also learned that no single department has a lock on innovation. The contest enabled us to tap into the knowledge and creativity of our employee base. Our people have great ideas, and we gave them the opportunity and the resources to show what they can do."**

Project Launchpad was so successful that it inspired a similar approach for solving challenges in modeling actuarial data, an area of critical focus in the insurance business. The company assembled a cross-functional team to look beyond the traditional solutions and develop innovative ways for handling increasingly complex data.

"After Project Launchpad demonstrated that our employees could help us solve problems like managing mobile computing, we realized we could use a similar approach to solve different kinds of problems, such as data modeling," Allan says. "The point of the story is that you don't always have to spend an arm and a leg on innovation. You can find great ideas by reaching into your organization and letting people work on projects that excite them."

Incentivizing Innovation

Let's stay on the topic of innovation a bit longer. In this section, I'd like to drill down and explore the process of encouraging and rewarding innovative behaviors and instilling a culture of innovation.

Becky Blalock is the former senior vice president and chief information officer at Atlanta-based Southern Company. With 4.4 million customers and more than 42,000 megawatts of generating capacity, Southern Company is the premier energy provider in the Southeast. A leading U.S. producer of electricity, Southern Company owns electric utilities in four states and a growing competitive generation company, as well as fiber optics and wireless communications. Its brands are known for excellent customer service, high reliability, and retail electric prices that are below the national average. The company is consistently listed among the top U.S. electric service providers in customer satisfaction by the American Customer Satisfaction Index and topped Fortune's "Most Admired" list in the electric and gas utility sector for 2011.

I cite these statistics and achievements to give you an idea of what makes Southern Company different from other companies in the energy sector. Southern Company doesn't see itself as just another utility. It sees itself as a company providing essential services to customers spread across four states. When tornados struck in Alabama, for example, Southern Company used Twitter to send updates to customers in affected areas. That might not seem like a big deal, but if you are a customer with no power, seeing a tweet on your smart phone that lets you know the repair trucks are on the way can bring a lot of comfort.

Becky fit in well with the customer-focused culture at Southern Company. In her role as CIO, she directed IT strategy and operations across the 120,000 square miles and nine subsidiaries of Southern Company. She led more than 1,100 employees, and her responsibilities encompassed infrastructure, networks, desktops, applications, telephony, and cyber security.

Technically, she's not really a techie. Becky has an undergraduate degree in business administration from State University of West Georgia. She holds a master's degree with honors in business administration from Mercer University, and she successfully completed the Program for Management Development at Harvard University in 1994. A graduate of Leadership Atlanta and Leadership Georgia, she was named a Fellow of the International Women's Forum Leadership Foundation.

Over the span of her career, Becky has served in a variety of leadership positions in corporate communication, external affairs, the office of the CEO, accounting, finance, and customer service. Prior to joining Southern Company, she was vice president of Georgia Power's community and economic development department, responsible for marketing and positioning the state of Georgia in a global economy. Under her leadership the department was internationally recognized as one of the top economic development organizations in the world, and she was named one of the "Top 10 Outstanding Young Leaders in Economic Development in America."

Becky has received a host of honors, including being named one of *Computerworld* magazine's 2006 Premier 100 IT Leaders and 2003 Georgia CIO of the Year, Global Category, by the Georgia CIO Leadership Association.

I mention Becky's accomplishments and awards because they are relevant. In today's complex and customer-centric markets, being technically proficient is not enough. You need to understand the needs of the business, and you need to understand the needs of the markets that the business serves.

Visualizing the customer and understanding the customer's needs is now part of the CIO's core responsibility. In the past, it might have been okay for the CIO to focus primarily on technology. Today, the CIO's vision must include the company's customers.

Southern Company, for example, is one of the nation's most automated energy providers. It uses automation to improve efficiency (internally) and to improve service to its customers (externally). The company is now applying its expertise in automation to the product itself—electric power. Southern Company is leveraging its automation capabilities to develop a Smart Grid that senses trouble and enables the company to take action to prevent potential outages and reduce the impact of outages when they do occur. From an internal perspective, it means rolling fewer trucks and deploying fewer repair teams. From an external perspective, it means higher levels of customer satisfaction.

The ability to balance a company's internal needs with the needs of its customers is becoming increasingly critical to the CIO's overall success. But achieving this balance is not a solo act. It requires company-wide effort and cooperation.

It also requires a culture of continuous innovation, because the needs of the market are continuously changing. Becky and her team at Southern Company were acutely aware of this, and they developed a unique process for encouraging and incentivizing innovation.

> **"Companies don't innovate—people do. If you want to be innovative as a company, you have to reward people for being innovative."**

I interviewed Becky while she was CIO, and she explained to me how the process works:

Companies don't innovate—people do. If you want to be innovative as a company, you have to reward people for being innovative. Seven years ago we created our intellectual property program. Anybody who turns in an idea gets a coin that says, "Innovative Thinker." Some people have 20 coins in their office.

Since inception, our employees have generated 500 ideas. About 10 percent of those ideas have cleared the hurdle for a conventional patent filing. Upon filing for a conventional patent, each employee inventor is awarded $500. If the patent is granted, each employee inventor gets $2,000. If we commercialize a patented idea, the inventors can receive up to 1 percent of the revenue. So far, the program has resulted in eight patents and brought in more than $12 million. It's also a great source of pride for all of us.

We recently licensed the rights to a product we developed through the program. The product is called EM-PACT^TM and it enables us to onboard contractors much more quickly than in the past. Another product developed through the program enables us to locate and recover missing meters. We're moving forward to obtain a patent on that, too.

IT presents an Innovator of the Year Award, and we make a big deal out of it. We produce a video about the winner and they receive $1,000. When people know they will be rewarded for innovating, they get excited and they start thinking about innovation. They focus on it. Even the coins help. They cost us three dollars apiece, but they mean a lot to people.

For the last five years, we have been ranked on Computerworld's list of "Best Places to Work in IT." This year we received our best ranking to date: number 18! Part of the reason for our ranking is due to the intellectual property program. We are seen as an innovative company. To celebrate this success, we create postcards for our employees. On one side it says, "Southern Company—One of the 100 Best Places to Work." On the other side, I write a note thanking the person for what they've done to help us make this a great place.

All of these steps create a positive culture. When you walk around our offices, you can see the postcards tacked up all over. People like them. The coins and the postcards are very effective symbols. They remind us of our commitment to innovation and excellence.

"When people know they will be rewarded for innovating, they get excited and they start thinking about innovation. They focus on it."

I think Becky's story is a powerful reminder of the importance of providing tangible rewards for innovation. Everyone wants to be recognized for making a contribution—it's simply human nature. Investing time and effort to devise a formal program for incentivizing innovation will surely pay dividends.

Chapter 4

Finding the Right Balance

In my numerous conversations with CIOs and other senior executives, several themes emerged. One of the most common themes was the importance of establishing an appropriate right balance between efficiency and innovation. As Randy Spratt suggested earlier, it's difficult to find the right balance when conditions around you are continually changing.

I agree with Randy, and with his idea of replacing the "perpetual pendulum" with a "virtuous cycle." But the essential challenge remains: How do you set your priorities when the ground under your feet is shifting? Today's markets move with breathtaking velocity. Maybe instead of striving to find the right balance, we should settle for a state of dynamic equilibrium.

But dynamic equilibrium wouldn't satisfy our need for ever increasing productivity and efficiency. That's why I like Randy's "virtuous cycle" approach to transformation. It leaves the door open for all kinds of changes.

The truth is that change comes in many shapes and sizes. Some changes are anticipated, some are unanticipated. One

CIO told me that he prefers intentional change over un-intentional change, but that's a little bit like saying that you don't like surprises.

Like it or not, the life of a CIO is spent managing change. Two decades ago, most equipment lasted five years. Until fairly recently, the average CIO could count on a three-year refresh cycle. Today, the refresh cycle is much quicker. The operating systems of some devices (such as mobile tablets) are updated twice annually, which means the CIO has six months to sit on his or her laurels before all hell breaks loose.

If the trend continues—and there's no sign that it will stop anytime soon—IT will be asked to support devices that are updated every 90 days.

This is not a trivial issue. Everyone, from the chairman of the board to the millennial you hired fresh out of college, expects full network connectivity from his or her favorite devices. If you can't provide the connectivity they demand, you will hear from them.

Today, and for the foreseeable future, it's BYOD—bring your own device. Yes, there will be a seemingly endless series of integration issues, but woe to the CIO who can't manage them all smoothly.

If it's any comfort, this challenge of managing change and productivity has been around for a while. Economists even have a name for it: the productivity frontier. The productivity frontier is where you create maximum value for the company by leveraging the best available technologies and management techniques.

Back in the good old days, the productivity frontier inched forward. You worried about it every five years. Then as the pace of technology development accelerated, you worried about it every three years. Now you have to worry about it every year, unless your sales force is using some kind of ultra-chic mobile tablets, in which case you might have to worry about it every quarter.

Winds of Change

Stephen Gold is a smart, savvy executive. He's senior vice president and chief information officer at Avaya, a global leader in business communications systems. Before joining Avaya, he held similar senior-level posts at Merck and Medco. It's fair to say that when it comes to IT strategy and leadership, Stephen is a great source of information and insight.

Recently I asked Stephen for his opinion on the changing role and responsibility of the CIO. "I think that some subtle, but important shifts have occurred in the past two years," Stephen told me. "Three or four years ago, the CIO's mandate was biased toward efficiency, cost savings, optimization, and streamlining business operations, both inside the IT organization and across the enterprise. Today, the winds have shifted. CIOs are still expected to drive efficiency through innovation, but they're also expected to drive revenue and value for the business."

''Today, the winds have shifted. CIOs are still expected to drive efficiency through innovation, but they're also expected to drive revenue and value for the business.''

The idea of the CIO as a "value enabler" is not entirely new. But Stephen has hit the bull's-eye by pointing out that in today's modern global enterprise, the CIO is now expected to help the business generate value and grow revenue. In other words, being perceived as a "value enabler" is no longer merely a compliment—it's rapidly becoming a basic part of the CIO's mandate.

It also means that to an increasing degree, IT is becoming responsible for creating and enabling real business value. When you think about it, all of this represents an amazing evolution for the IT department. A mere five years ago, IT was still regarded as the people you call when your printer stops working. Now, IT is perceived as an integral part of the corporate revenue engine. This is true progress, for IT and the enterprise.

Of course, the elevated role of the CIO and the IT function means greater responsibilities and a heavier workload. That translates into more projects, faster turnaround times, tighter deadlines, and higher expectations. It also requires getting accustomed to a different set of metrics. Until fairly recently, the CIO was mostly concerned with driving efficiency, and the metrics reflected that bias. Today, as the CIO becomes more involved in the value creation process, the metrics are more likely to focus on revenue, market share, growth, cost of sales, and other measures commonly associated with "the business."

And this raises another interesting question: When are we going to stop referring to IT and "the business" as separate entities? I think it's time to agree that IT is a critical part of "the business," and that, together, we're all parts of the larger enterprise. The mission of IT and the mission of "the business" is the same: to ensure the growth and viability of the enterprise.

The transformational CIO understands and embraces this common mission and shared purpose. Like the captain of a ship, the transformational CIO senses the winds of change and responds appropriately to maintain a steady course.

The Third Bucket

All of the CIOs interviewed for this book agreed that operational excellence and innovation are two prime areas in which success is imperative.

But there is a third area in which some CIOs will be expected to excel: customer management. This third area—or third bucket, if you will—is becoming increasingly important as products and services become increasingly dependent on technology. If what you're selling is technology, it makes perfect sense for the CIO to be involved in the customer management process.

To be fair, I think we're mostly talking about business-to-business (B2B) scenarios here, in which the CIO is brought into a meeting with a customer or prospective customer for the purpose of helping the sales executives accelerate the sales process or close a deal.

But the CIO can also help sales and marketing teams explain the value of sophisticated technologies. After all, a prospective customer is likely to view the CIO as a credible expert in technology—especially when the CIO's company is actually using the products or services being sold.

The idea of the customer-facing CIO makes more sense in some situations than in others. If the product you offer is primarily intended for consumers—take the Apple iPhone, for example—then you don't need to include the CIO in the sales process.

But when the product or service is highly complex and technology-dependent—let's say it's a pharmacy benefits management service or a data security management service—then it makes good business sense to bring the CIO into the sales process.

Not every CIO will feel comfortable taking on a sales role. But some CIOs tell me that they enjoy their customer-facing responsibilities because interacting with customers gives them a much better understanding of the world that exists outside of the IT organization.

That improved level of understanding helps him do a better job of serving the company's customers, which in turn, helps the company. All told, it's a great example of a virtuous circle in which the CIO plays a critical role.

The Closer

I had a wonderful conversation with Kim Hammonds, vice president of IT Infrastructure at The Boeing Company. Kim told me a great story supporting the idea of customer-focused technology executives.

First, some background: As most of you know, Boeing is the world's largest aerospace company and leading manufacturer of commercial jetliners and defense, space, and security systems. As a top U.S. exporter, Boeing supports airlines and U.S. and allied government customers in more than 90 countries. The company is organized into two business units: Boeing Commercial Airplanes and Boeing Defense, Space & Security.

In 2010, Boeing's UK subsidiary, Boeing Defence UK, was competing for an important contract for the Log NEC program with the UK Ministry of Defence's Joint Support Chain, and reached back to the United States, asking IT to join the competition team. Here's the story, just the way Kim told me:

> *The ministry was looking to upgrade and transform its logistics systems, and it needed to upgrade the IT infrastructure supporting its logistics processes. We became part of the sales effort to win that contract for Boeing.*
>
> *We took the customer through our data centers and showed them how we migrate applications to those centers. We showed them how our logistics applications work and how we use our technology every day to support Boeing. We went through our processes in detail, so they could see for themselves how we use the systems and why we have such confidence in our technology. It was a fantastic experience, for us and for the customer.*

We ended up winning the contract, and it was a very big win for all of us. One of the company's strategic objectives is increasing sales in the international market, and so it certainly helped our overall strategy.

And we were proud that IT played a role in securing business growth from an important market. I think it shows the direction the world is moving, and it highlights the role of the CIO as an executive who leads the IT organization and supports the company's growth engines.

We have tremendous technical capabilities within the four walls of this company . . . it makes sense for IT to partner with the business units, and support the company's efforts to win new business and compete more effectively in world markets.

Kim also told me the key to working with the business is developing "a deeply rooted understanding of the business and the challenges facing the business . . . you need that deep understanding so you can figure out the best way of applying technology to generate business value and competitive advantages."

> " . . . it makes sense for IT to partner with the business units, and support the company's efforts to win new business and compete more effectively in world markets."

I think that her words really capture the transformational CIO's pivotal role as a driver of business growth and value in the modern corporation.

Outside versus Inside

Early in the process of writing this book, I interviewed Tony Scott, the CIO of Microsoft. Tony has had an illustrious career, holding executive posts at General Motors and Disney. You will hear more from Tony in later chapters of the book, but I wanted to share an observation that he mentioned during our conversation.

Here's the gist of what he said: In the past, when Microsoft delivered its software in physical form, the quality of the media (e.g., how many disks are defective?) and the quality of the packaging (e.g., container, printed materials) would be concerns, as well as any possible defects and bugs in the software itself. In other words, when Microsoft distributed its software, it also paid attention to the quality of the aluminized polycarbonate plastic CD-ROMs on which the software was inscribed, the packaging it was shipped in, and the printed documentation that accompanied each shipment.

The quality of the CD-ROMs, the packaging, and the documentation *had* to be a major focus, since there was really no other way to distribute software before broadband connections to the Internet became widely available.

But when the tipping point was reached and most of Microsoft's customers had high-speed Internet connections, the company could focus more of its energy on what really mattered, which was the quality of the user experience. This was truly a paradigm shift.

As the corporation shifted gears, the CIO's role also changed. Essentially, Microsoft transformed itself from a manufacturer of software into a marketer of software. That's a huge difference.

In previous times, the CIO's attention was focused almost exclusively on internal challenges. Today, the CIO's attention is divided between internal and external challenges.

"You have to pay attention to the company's customer base," says Tony. "You have to be aware of how the market perceives the company's products. If you're not conscious of external perceptions, you can do the wrong thing when you design and architect your IT infrastructure. Even if you get the internal processes right, you can do the wrong thing in terms of the market if you're not paying attention to what the market wants."

The modern CIO has to be "an inside person and an outside person," says Tony. "You have to be perceptive about external and internal influences. And then you have to find a balance between the two."

> "You have to be aware of how the market perceives the company's products. If you're not conscious of external perceptions, you can do the wrong thing when you design and architect your IT infrastructure. Even if you get the internal processes right, you can do the wrong thing in terms of the market if you're not paying attention to what the market wants."

Articulating the Value of Technology

The rapid evolution of markets and the consumerization of technology have combined to create a "new normal" at the modern enterprise. Today, everyone expects their devices to be connected, compatible, and secure. They expect the technology they use at work to have the same user-friendly features as the technology they use at home or in the car.

They see technology as part of the company's competitive arsenal, and they cannot imagine trying to compete without it. From their perspective, new technology is like "table stakes" in poker—you need it to stay in the game.

In a world in which technology has become increasingly commoditized, the role of the CIO shifts from technology provider to value enabler. For many CIOs, this represents a difficult transition. Making the leap from technology guru to business partner isn't easy. In addition to understanding the business, you also need to make sure that the business understands you. In other words, you need to communicate in terms that business people understand.

My good friend Ramón Baez, the VP and CIO at Kimberly-Clark, has become an expert in communicating with the business. And he believes firmly that most IT leaders need to sharpen their communication skills.

"Everyone in IT should be able to articulate the value of what we do in clear business language," says Ramón. "It's incumbent on the CIO and the CIO's deputies to develop the skills they need to communicate with the business."

> **"Everyone in IT should be able to articulate the value of what we do in clear business language."**

Explaining the benefits—and drawbacks—of new technology can be problematic, especially in situations where the new technology is replacing an older and more familiar technology.

For example, the company recently considered using a cloud-based human resources solution. Ramón and his team knew that it was important for the company's business leaders to see the value of moving from a traditional HR system to a cloud-based service. But they weren't convinced that the vendor's sales team could explain the pros and cons of the cloud to the business leaders.

Essentially, Ramón used his own communication skills to teach the vendors how to communicate to the C-suite. Here's the story in his own words:

We did a dry run with me, the head of HR, and the vendor's team. They did their normal presentation and we realized very quickly that it wouldn't fly with our C-suite. So we told them what our top executives needed to see. We told them, "If you're the CEO or the head of a region, here's the kind of information you're looking for, here's how you can use the new system to manage overtime costs, here's how you can search through the new system to find employees with special skills, here's how you can figure out the optimal ways for utilizing contingent labor."

You see, the vendor's team knew their system inside and out, but they didn't know what was important to us. We needed to communicate to the vendor what was important to our company. We had to show them how to present to our company. That's the magic, the secret sauce—knowing what's important.

And that's why it's critical for the CIO to really understand what's important to the company from a business perspective—so you can explain it to all the people who are going to help you become a truly transformational leader. You can't do it alone, so you need to make sure that everyone understands what the business needs.

It's not about the technology. It's about the problem we're trying to solve. It's about the value we generate. It's about making a better company.

"It's not about the technology. It's about the problem we're trying to solve. It's about the value we generate. It's about making a better company."

Part of the ongoing challenge is redefining the traditional IT perspective on innovation. When the role of IT was confined largely to back-office operations, everything—including innovation—was looked at through the lens of operational efficiency. So when you talked to someone from IT about innovation, you were usually talking about improving some aspect of the company's back office.

In today's customer-centric economy, IT is expected to drive innovation for the front office as well as the back office. "We are no longer just innovating for IT," says Ramón. "We're innovating for sales, for marketing—and for our customers. That's the biggest change from the past. We're not just focused on productivity and the bottom line. We're also very focused on the top line."

That doesn't mean that IT has forgotten about productivity. It's just that IT views productivity more broadly than it did in the past. "We want to help our sales teams be more productive and more effective so they can really dazzle their customers," says Ramón. If that means tweaking newly released mobile tablets for an important sales presentation, IT will get the job done.

From my perspective, the willingness to work closely with the company's business leaders and stay abreast of their concerns is one of the key qualities that elevates Ramón into the ranks of genuinely transformational CIOs. It has also helped him become a global ambassador for Kimberly-Clark. "My boss feels comfortable with me talking about the company in front of external audiences and he sees the value in it," says Ramón.

Chapter 5

The Customer-Focused CIO

Back in the 1990s, terms like "customer-centric" and "customer focused" were invoked to describe marketing strategies based on satisfying the needs and desires of real customers. After decades of product-centric marketing strategies, the idea of building marketing strategies around what customers really wanted seemed positively revolutionary!

Today, the idea of customer centricity seems like a no-brainer. We are surrounded by examples of successful companies with customer-centric business models: Apple, Amazon, Best Buy, Dell, eBay, and Google, to name just a few.

For a while, though, it seemed as though the trend would be limited to customer-facing operations such as sales and marketing. Gradually, however, it has proliferated across the enterprise. Just recently, I had the pleasure of speaking with Steve Phillips, senior vice president and chief information officer at Avnet, one of the world's largest distributors of electronic components.

Steve described an initiative called Avnet Express, a dedicated e-commerce portal developed by the IT team to reach a specific group of desirable engineering customers. Here's the story in brief:

Avnet's existing e-commerce capabilities were built to enable traditional business-to-business (B2B) selling scenarios. That was fine for most customers. But a certain segment of the customer base needed an e-commerce portal that delivered more of a business-to-consumer (B2C) type of experience. This customer segment was made up mostly of designers—people who needed small numbers of components for building prototypes.

The existing system was designed for larger-scale transactions, and nothing was shipped until a full credit check was performed, which is standard operating procedure in many B2B situations.

But if you're building and testing prototypes, you need components quickly and with the fewest possible hassles. So Avnet's IT team developed a B2B portal for the designers that looks and feels more like a B2C portal.

"We make it easy for them to purchase the components they need, and we offer them next-day shipping. It is very practical, for them and for us," says Steve. "What's really been interesting is that we've had to learn about user-friendly B2C selling techniques—we had to learn about intelligent search, online chat, enabled shopping lists, and other capabilities that make it easier for customer to buy from us. Our epiphany was to treat these customers like B2C customers, even though they are technically B2B customers. We realized that their expectations had been shaped by sites like Amazon, and we had to create a similar experience."

The result of this extra effort has been truly spectacular—the site saw one-year revenue growth of nearly 200 percent in 2010.

Another incredible benefit: The new e-commerce portal had no negative impact on existing sales. In other words, it was mostly all new revenue, with no cannibalization.

I really like Steve's story because it opens up a new dimension for IT. Instead of being purely focused on meeting internal needs, IT gets to stretch beyond the limits of its traditional boundaries and focus on generating real value for the business. After all, what can be more valuable than a satisfied customer?

Top Line or Bottom Line?

My interviews with Kim Hammonds and Steve Phillips reminded me of a friend who liked to say that no company can save its way to greatness. He had worked at a large media company that had essentially driven itself into mediocrity through a strategy of continuous cost reduction. In the short term, the strategy worked. Profits soared. The company became the darling of Wall Street and its management was praised as "visionary."

I'm sure you can see where this story is going. The company's most creative and successful executives left. The quality of the company's products declined. As a result, the company lost market share. Sales revenue declined. Profits declined. The company was eventually acquired by a competitor and dismantled.

My friend's story illustrates the danger of focusing so much on the bottom line that you forget about the top line. Why do companies exist? To make money. How do they make money? By selling products or services—many companies sell both products *and* services. Who buys what companies sell? Customers. That's why customers are important—they make the cash register ring.

Customers generate sales revenue, and sales revenue—the top line—is the lifeblood of all companies. You can't have a bottom line unless there's a top line first. Any executive who thinks the top line is "someone else's problem" is missing the whole point of why the company exists. The company does not exist to create efficiency—the company exists to make money, and the way you make money is by selling products and services that customers want to buy.

This brings us back to a central question: What is the appropriate role of the CIO in a modern organization that competes in a rapidly changing global economy?

Driving Business Growth

My good friend Tim Crawford is vice president of information technology and chief information officer at All Covered, a division of Konica-Minolta Business Solutions USA. Tim has spoken at several of my CIO Executive Leadership events, and his message is always clear: Transformational CIOS don't just "create value" for the enterprise, they drive revenue.

Tim is careful about making the distinction between activities that result in bottom-line gains and activities that focus on the top line. For the past decade, CIOs have been expected to focus primarily on driving down costs and leveraging technology to make common business practices more efficient. There is no question that efficiency is an important way to create value for the business, but that's not what Tim is talking about.

When Tim talks about creating value, he literally means helping the business sell more products and services to its customers. In other words, he's talking about growing the value of the customer base. He's talking about the CIO contributing to the top line, in addition to improving the bottom line.

For many IT departments, this implies a radical shift in perception. For years, IT departments have been trained to see internal users of IT as "customers." There's nothing wrong with that—most people would rather be thought of as "customers" rather than "users"—but it constricts the range of IT to a very limited universe of internal "customers."

Ideally, the IT department should see its customer base as a combination of internal customers *and* external customers. The internal customers are the traditional consumers of corporate IT services. But the external customers are really the company's customers—all those wonderful people who pay money for whatever it is that the company sells to generate revenue.

This might seem simplistic, but it's a key point of differentiation between traditional IT strategy and *transformational IT strategy.*

Transformational IT strategy is informed and guided by the understanding that IT should add value internally (through greater efficiency) and externally (through increased revenue). Greater efficiency contributes to the bottom line; increased revenue contributes to the top line.

Okay, now it's probably fair to ask: Is all value created equal? Is a penny saved really equal to a penny earned? In other words, should the CIO focus on the bottom line, the top line, or both? Is there a formula for determining the right balance?

There isn't a scientific formula—at least not today. The appropriate balance will depend on the company's strategy, the market, the wider economy, and a host of other variables. It does seem certain, however, that the CIO will be expected to become an active participant in discussions that focus on growing the business. That's a big change from the past, and it requires a different view of how value is created, both internally and externally.

The Rapid Enabler

As Randy Spratt suggested earlier, it's all about finding the right balance. It's not a contest of top line *versus* bottom line, because you need both to succeed.

It's also important to remember that no two companies are exactly alike, so every company will have to find its own balance. The idea of balance also applies to the strategic role of the CIO. In many companies, the CIO can contribute significantly to the company's long-term success by focusing primarily on enablement and support.

This became clear to me after my conversation with Brian Bonner, the CIO at Texas Instruments. Brian is a graduate of the Fuqua School of Business at Duke University, and before becoming TI's global CIO, he was the company's vice president of analog acquisition integrations. In other words, he was one of the guys responsible for making sure that TI's mergers and acquisitions (M&A) strategy was successful.

Integrating the assets and resources of a newly acquired company is not an easy task—just ask anyone who's tried. Doing it successfully—not just once, but many times—really puts you in a league of your own. That's one of the reasons I believe that Brian's point of view, based on his own experiences, is so valuable.

Brian doesn't believe that every CIO has to be transformational. In most cases, says Brian, being genuinely helpful to the business is more than enough. For the CIO, being genuinely helpful means really understanding what the business needs and how the business operates. It also means understanding how products and services produced or distributed by the business are used by its customers.

Different businesses have different strategies and different operating models. When the strategy is sound and the operational model is sturdy, the CIO's job is to support the status quo. As the saying goes—if it ain't broke, don't fix it. The CIO is still responsible for optimizing, streamlining, and improving business processes. In most instances, fine-tuning an existing process can be more helpful—and less disruptive—to the business than a full-scale transformation project.

Texas Instruments (TI) designs and manufactures analog and digital semiconductors and integrated circuits. TI serves 80,000 customers worldwide, helping them deliver consumer and industrial electronics products with greater performance, increased power efficiency, higher precision, more mobility, and better quality.

"We've got a good strategy here and we're clicking along and executing on it," says Brian. "We focus on rapid enablement. When the business has a good idea, we try to enable it rapidly. When we come up with an innovation that will help the business, we apply it very quickly. We are more closely aligned with the concepts of operational effectiveness and organizational development than with transformation."

> "We focus on rapid enablement. When the business has a good idea, we try to enable it rapidly. When we come up with an innovation that will help the business, we apply it very quickly."

In our conversation, Brian cited the Hedgehog Concept described by Jim Collins in *Good to Great*. I was delighted to hear that, since *Good to Great* is one of my favorite business books. It has stood the test of time, and Jim's words are still very relevant. Here's an excerpt of Jim's writing:

> *The essence of a Hedgehog Concept is to attain piercing clarity about how to produce the best long-term results, and then exercising the relentless discipline to say, "No thank you" to opportunities that fail the hedgehog test. When we examined the Hedgehog Concepts of the good-to-great companies, we found they reflected deep understanding of three intersecting circles: (1) what you are deeply passionate about, (2) what you can be the best in the world at, and (3) what best drives your economic engine.*

From Brian's perspective, not every company needs a CIO whose main focus is continuous transformation. If your company's business model is built on delivering a durable, high-quality product that is difficult to design and manufacture, then it probably makes sense to focus more on operational efficiency and organizational development than on transformation.

Brian also suggests that it's time for people to stop wondering if the CIO has earned "a seat at the executive table."

"If they think you can help, you will be invited to the meeting," he says.

Own, Rent, or Both?

My friend Joe Weinman leads the communications, media, and entertainment segment for Hewlett-Packard's Worldwide Industry Solutions. His team spans the Americas, Europe, Middle East, Africa, Asia Pacific, Japan, and Australia.

Within the cloud computing community, however, he is best known as the founder of *Cloudonomics*, a rigorous discipline that combines business, technology, strategy, and economics. Although no stranger to technology—Joe is an accomplished inventor with 14 patents awarded—he is considered one of the world's leading experts on the business value of the cloud.

Joe notes that the valuation of cloud computing solutions was initially focused on cost reduction, and then later on business agility. "The term 'business agility' sounds like a good thing, but it needs to be more quantitative to be a useful criterion," says Joe. "Moreover, 'cost' is not a simple metric, and there are more business metrics that are useful—many of which are surprisingly difficult to quantify, especially when you are trying to pursue the correct decision for your business."

> **"The term 'business agility' sounds like a good thing, but it needs to be more quantitative to be a useful criterion."**

He also contends that much of the conventional wisdom on the cloud is flawed. "There is a theory that public cloud computing is the end-state for all IT, and that the enterprise data center is on the way out." But Joe argues that, for a variety of reasons, the future is much more likely to have a mix of owned resources used in combination with public services.

"People own cars and rent them, they own houses and stay in hotels, they have kitchens and they eat out in restaurants. Generally, a mix of owned, dedicated resources and pay-per-use services is the norm." Moreover, Joe says, this blend is not based on some "variety is the spice of life" platitude, but on inescapable, rational, quantitative economics.

The best-known proponent of the "all IT will move to the cloud" argument is probably Nicholas Carr. He argues that in the same way that virtually all electricity comes from the "public" grid, rather than "private, on-premises generation," virtually all IT will come from the "public cloud, rather than private, on-premises data centers."

Joe points out, however, that electric utilities not only do have economies of scale, but often have zero cost of goods sold: The Hoover Dam doesn't pay for each gallon of water or its latent kinetic and potential energy. Those economies of scale, and the lack of convenient distributed solutions, mean that even after accounting for transmission and distribution energy (and hard dollar) losses, and margin, selling, general and administration (SG&A) expenses, uncollectible accounts, and the like, the electric utility still offers a compelling value proposition for most customers. However, large power-hungry enterprises still do generate their own electricity, and emerging technologies such as home solar panels and fuel cells are likely to tip the balance back to private generation.

A better analogy, Joe argues, is the decision between owning (or financing or leasing) a car and renting one. "A new intermediate car probably costs about three hundred dollars per month, either in lease, finance, or depreciation. That's ten dollars a day. Try renting that same car for that amount." Joe points out that even a large public service provider, such as Avis or Hertz, may charge three to five times that, even though they should have a roughly similar cost structure— volume discounts, statistical effects, and so on—as a public cloud provider.

The first lesson is that a service provider may cost substantially more for a given unit of resource than owning it yourself. The second lesson, however, is that paying more can still be a good deal: a rational economic decision. If you use a car every day, it's probably cheaper to own one. But if you need transportation only every once in a while, it's probably cheaper to rent a car or take a taxi.

"The optimal decision is very dependent on the usage profile," he says. Frequent, unvarying use tends to favor an ownership model. Variable, unpredictable use tends to favor a short-term rental model. Even though the unit cost of the "rental" may be higher, it is the total cost of the solution within a planning horizon that should be the key choice-point.

Multiple Models

In cloud computing, a variety of models are in use. Netflix, for example, has moved all of its IT to the cloud, including encoding and over-the-top on-demand video. But Zynga uses the public cloud only in the early days of a new game; once demand has flattened, it moves the workload back in-house, to the so-called "Z cloud" private cloud. Other companies use in-house resources for core or traditional workloads, while using the cloud for (highly intermittent) testing and development.

Joe Weinman says that questions such as "Will all IT move to the public cloud?" or "Is the cloud overhyped?" are the wrong questions for CIOs to ask. Instead, CIOs should be evaluating their current and planned enterprise application architecture and determining which components should be where and why.

"Moreover," Joe says, "unless you are a start-up, costs to rewrite code or migrate applications and users need to be factored into the decision." And, except for unique business functions where IT is a source of competitive advantage, you should be looking to software-as-a-service (SaaS) providers where possible.

"Coding applications yourself goes far beyond the owner-ship/rental decision for infrastructure. It's like designing and manufacturing your own personal car." A vehicle from one of the standard providers will probably meet most people's needs just fine, especially now that most SaaS providers offer a high degree of customizability on top of the base platform.

There are other benefits to using the cloud than just helping to optimize total cost. One benefit is the ability to compress time without paying a premium. Because resources are priced on a pay-per-use basis, one thousand server-hours costs the same whether it is one server for a thousand hours or a thousand servers for an hour. "To the extent that an application is highly parallelizable, the public cloud gives you something for nothing: the power to speed up results without paying a penny more," says Joe.

> **"To the extent that an application is highly parallelizable, the public cloud gives you something for nothing: the power to speed up results without paying a penny more."**

A good example is when the *Washington Post* converted Hillary Clinton's schedule from a nonsearchable PDF of over 17,000 pages to a searchable archive, within hours, at a cost of less than a hundred and fifty dollars. Virtually any company can benefit from this "free time compression," offering compelling strategic advantages in competitive markets.

Also Consider the User Experience

Yet another often overlooked business benefit of the cloud is an improved customer and user experience. "Commercially, an increasing portion of the economy is based on either on-line ordering or online delivery, and internally, online applications, whether mobile or desktop, are a foundation of labor productivity." This includes everything from e-commerce and e-auctions to e-books and tablet applications. In the enterprise, it may include contact center applications, white-collar applications, mobile asset tracking, or mobile field force applications to manufacturing applications.

In a commercial context, Joe notes that delays have been shown to directly impact revenue: Google has determined that a few hundred milliseconds of extra page load time result in 20 percent fewer clickthroughs, directly resulting in a 20 percent revenue decrease. Joe argues that "today's highly interactive applications require a geographically dispersed infrastructure to reach a global customer and user base." Consequently, having server and storage resources deployed around the globe running interactive applications is key.

Here again, Joe argues that the cloud can give you something for nothing. "Rather than expending scarce capital to build a data center in every region, or in every country, it's much more cost-effective to use the cloud for content and application delivery. If you use FedEx, UPS, or DHL for delivering physical content today, you already appreciate the benefit of leveraging services available from a provider with a global footprint. The public cloud does the same thing for virtual content."

In summary, Joe says he does not have a deeply seated belief in favor of or against the public cloud: "Enterprise data centers and cloud service providers each have a role to play. The important thing is to understand your business, appreciate the variety of benefits that the cloud can offer, and determine how best to integrate this new option into your overall strategy."

> "Rather than expending scarce capital to build a data center in every region, or in every country, it's much more cost-effective to use the cloud for content and application delivery."

Chapter 6

To Cloud or Not to Cloud

To cloud or not to cloud? That is *not* the question. We can't avoid the issue of cloud computing because cloud computing is already here. And we can't spend endless time arguing and agonizing over cloud computing. The business expects results, and it doesn't really care whether we use the cloud or not to deliver those results.

So let's just agree that the cloud is not a "one size fits all" solution, that the cloud is not a complete solution, and that every company will eventually have to develop its own unique cloud strategy.

There is no standard process. No college or university today offers a course in cloud migration. It's a new field, and the CIOs that I interviewed for this book are working hard to figure out the best ways for leveraging the cloud to generate value for the businesses they support.

Pat Toole is a general manager in IBM's technology services business. Before moving into this role, Pat was IBM's CIO. As CIO, he helped IBM navigate into the cloud.

In addition to being a major provider of cloud services, IBM is also a major user of cloud services. Part of Pat's responsibility as CIO was determining which services and capabilities to move into the cloud. I asked him to summarize his advice for CIOs who are trying to chart a course through cloud territory. Here is what he told me:

Every so often in this industry, something comes along that seems to generate its own momentum. The move to client-server technology was an example of that kind of trend. It just hit us by storm, and you felt that if you weren't doing something to move from mainframe to client-server, you probably weren't doing something that you should be doing.

The truth is that you never want to get left behind when one of these big waves hits. Sure, there's a lot of hype. Some of the economics might not pan out the way you thought it would. Each company will have to wrestle with this in its own way to make sure that it provides the proper return on its investment.

When we consider moving a workload into the cloud, we look at three components. First we look at the current cost versus the target cost and the time it will take us to get there.

Second, we look at the actual cost of moving from the current model to the target model.

Third, we look at the potential benefits we will gain by moving that workload into the cloud. Will there be improved utilization? Will the labor costs be lower? Will there be a higher level of standardization?

All of this wraps up into our calculation of the cloud's value in terms of that workload. That's how we do "cloudonomics" here. We break it down into components that we can analyze. It's not rocket science, but it is computer science.

And we see the challenge from both ends, because we use cloud technology and we also provide services and products via cloud technology. It's very exciting for us to work on both sides of the cloud.

Pat says there's still low-hanging fruit in the cloud, but you have to know where to look:

You have to pick a point of entry where you can gain traction and be successful. Look first at application development testing, business analytics, collaboration, Web serving, and maybe virtual desktops. I would avoid areas like traditional ERP and financial management applications as entry points.

I think this is great advice from a guy who has been there *and* done that. In *The Transformational CIO*, I described how Pat made sure that IT was aligned with the company's earnings per share goals. I remember being impressed by his analytic approach to managing IT. I'm not surprised that he took a similarly analytic approach to managing the cloud.

Fail Fast, Fail Cheap

We've all heard the phrase, "Fail fast, fail cheap," but most of us tend to believe that it applies to someone else. Let's face it: Nobody wants to fail, so we spend most of our careers trying to avoid failure.

At the risk of sounding like some kind of New Age guru, it's important to remember that failure is the mother of success. We learn more from our mistakes than from our triumphs.

Thanks to modern technology, we can test our ideas much more rapidly and much less expensively than at any time in the past. Rapid prototyping is no longer an exotic process—it is becoming increasingly common. Fairly soon, it will be considered a standard methodology for developing new products and services. I recommend reading "A More Rational Approach to New-Product Development," an article published in the March 2008 edition of *Harvard Business Review*. Although the article focuses on new-product development in the pharmaceutical industry, the general concept it describes can apply to any competitive business.

Basically, the article suggests that it's better to divide the new-product development process into two stages: an early stage in which you evaluate potential and identify risks, and a second stage in which you actually move the new product or service closer to launch.

The goal of the first stage is "truth seeking" and quickly eliminating ideas that don't seem likely to succeed. Only ideas that survive this first stage are moved along into the second stage, where they are subjected to thorough evaluations.

The second stage is "success seeking," and it is more intensive—and considerably more expensive—than the first stage. The authors of the article suggest that the early stage costs are one-fifth to one-fiftieth the costs of later-stage testing. That's a significant difference, and it provides a good foundation for arguing in favor of using a staged approach.

While the two-stage strategy might seem like common sense, the truth is that many organizations take an "all or nothing" approach to testing new products and services. The traditional approach assumes that innovation is a "dark art" and not a process, and that it's best left to small groups of dedicated "innovators." In times past, when the speed of innovation was slower and markets were less fragmented, the old approach made sense. But it doesn't make sense today.

Separating new-product development into two discreet phases saves time and money, since the first phase is quicker and less expensive than the second phase. The two-stage approach also increases the chances of successful new-product launches, because ideas that are likely to succeed are identified earlier in the process. The traditional approach doesn't separate the winners from the losers until the end of the process. In today's hyper-competitive markets, the traditional approach seems both slow and risky.

A Skunk Works in the Cloud

For decades, the term "skunk works" was associated with Clarence "Kelly" L. Johnson, the legendary designer at Lockheed Aircraft Corporation. The skunk works legend is so powerful that the name has been trademarked and is now used officially by Lockheed Martin's Advanced Development Programs.

The group that became the Skunk Works® began in 1943 as a small team of young engineers within Lockheed. The team's initial assignment was developing a jet fighter that would counter the jets under development in Nazi Germany. Working in a rented circus tent, Johnson and his team broke practically every rule in the book. But they delivered the XP-80 Shooting Star—America's first jet fighter—in just 143 days.

The success of the XP-80 project led to more assignments. Over the years, the team designed and delivered famous airplanes such as the F-104 Starfighter, the U-2, the SR-71 Blackbird, the F-117 Nighthawk, and the F-22 Raptor.

Johnson's amazing team of innovators began work in a rented circus tent. Today, you can be innovative without leaving your office.

That's because the cloud is ideally suited for testing and evaluating new products and services. The cloud enables you to fail fast and fail cheap, because you don't have to buy anything except the capability you need to perform the test. You don't have to invest in new infrastructure or lots of new software—you buy exactly what you need to run the test and not a bit more.

With the cloud, you can create a real innovation pipeline, at far lower costs than ever before. This is the true value of the cloud—it's the least expensive test bed ever invented. In the old days, your skunk works had its own physical space, along with desks, furniture, equipment, support staff, and so on. Today, your skunk works can live in the cloud.

Weaving the Seamless Tapestry

I think it's appropriate to conclude this section of the book with a visit to Martin Davis, the executive vice president and head of technology integration at Wells Fargo. Davis and his team led the technology integration required after the merger of Wells Fargo and Wachovia. The merger created a financial services organization with 70 million banking customers, $1.3 trillion in assets, 275,000 employees, 80 lines of business, and more than 4,000 applications.

Weaving these strands together to form a seamless tapestry posed complex challenges, but as a seasoned veteran of previous mergers, Martin had the experience and the knowledge necessary to manage the process smoothly and successfully. Before heading the integration effort, he was CIO at Wachovia. Prior to that, he had served in a variety of executive roles at the bank, including SVP and group executive of Information Services Architecture and Administration; SVP and group manager of Capital Markets Technology; and SVP and group manager of Bankcard Technologies. In 2001, he helped oversee the Wachovia–First Union merger, which also involved a highly complex integration process.

Part of every integration challenge is identifying which systems to keep running and which systems to close down. In this regard, the Wells Fargo–Wachovia merger was no different. In some instances, it made more sense to keep the Wachovia system and shutter the Wells Fargo system. In other cases, the opposite was true.

But what elevated the integration process to truly Herculean proportions was its sheer size and scope. No single human can manage a project of that size, so team-work is absolutely essential. But you can't just *tell* people to work together; you need to give them common goals. Here's what Martin told me when I asked him about his leadership style:

> One of the key lessons I've learned over the past 26 years is that the more you can share the big picture with people, the more likely they are to succeed. When you think about the size and scale of our organization, it's critical for people to have a good sense of the big picture and the common purpose.
>
> Understanding the big picture enables us to innovate so quickly for our customers and improve the way we deliver services. I use the analogy of building a house. The plumber will do a better job if you show him plans for the entire house instead of just telling him that you want three bathrooms.
>
> From my vantage point as leader of the technology integration office, I can see how critical it is for everyone to know the master game plan and understand their role. There are a lot of moving parts. When you change something, you have to understand the impact of that change on parts of the company. It takes a lot of coordination.

> "Understanding the big picture enables us to innovate so quickly for our customers and improve the way we deliver services."

One of the ways Martin keeps up with the hectic pace of change is through a weekly report on the various changes taking place across the company's extensive IT portfolio:

We call it the "Airspace Analysis Report," and it really helps us keep the integration process running smoothly. Three teams look at the report, and they look for situations where an integration change could have an impact in their "air space." It's like being a flight controller—you want to keep the planes from colliding.

But at the end of the day, it's really all about teamwork. We're all focused on serving our customers and providing them with the financial services they need. That's our common purpose.

Martin used the word "customer" many times over the course of our conversation. His understanding of the big picture is crystal clear. And it made me reflect on how IT has evolved into a lot more than just a component of financial services.

Honestly, can you imagine a bank without IT? I think it's safe to say that in most instances, IT has become the primary product that banks deliver to their customers. When you use an ATM or pay a bill online or access your account balance from your mobile phone—that's an IT product you're tapping into.

So it's totally appropriate for the IT teams at Wells Fargo to think of their main job as serving the bank's external customers!

"But the winning financial institution will be the one that serves its customers best. When I wake up in the morning, I'm not thinking about what kind of new technology I should buy—I'm thinking about how we can serve our customers better."

Toward the end of our conversation, I asked Martin to list the main challenges facing IT executives in today's ultra-competitive financial services markets. Here's what he told me:

You have to attract the best talent. That's key, because you cannot execute unless you have great teams. And the ability to execute is absolutely critical in this industry.

But the winning financial institution will be the one that serves its customers best. When I wake up in the morning, I'm not thinking about what kind of new technology I should buy—I'm thinking about how we can serve our customers better. That's a different way of looking at the world. It's part of our culture here. It gives us a competitive advantage.

Part II

Driving Change

Chapter 7

In Front of the Firewall

Everyone, it seems, has their own view about the evolutionary stages of IT. It usually sounds something like this: First came the mainframe era, then the client-server era, then the PC era, then the Internet era, then the service-oriented architecture (SOA) era, then the cloud era . . .

But after speaking recently with Esat Sezer, I decided that you can collapse the history of IT into two major eras. Let's call them "The Era of IT Behind the Firewall" and "The Era of Converged Technologies."

The first epoch included the Age of the Mainframes and the Age of Distributed Computing. The new era—the one we're experiencing today—is marked by four transformational trends in computing: mobile, cloud, social, and big data.

Esat, as many of you know, is the senior vice president and CIO at Coca-Cola Enterprises, the third-largest Coca-Cola bottler in the world. Its beverage portfolio includes energy drinks, still and sparkling waters, juices, sports drinks, fruit drinks, coffee-based beverages, and teas. The company's markets include the United Kingdom, France, the Netherlands, Norway, and Sweden.

Esat was born, raised, and educated in Istanbul. Before joining Coca-Cola, he held senior IT management posts at Whirlpool, Colgate-Palmolive, and Andersen Consulting in London. I mention his bio because it shows that he's been around the block—and as a result of his experience, he has developed the keen perspective of a truly seasoned global technology executive. I value that perspective, and that's why I'm happy that Esat agreed to share his insights with us.

"For the first time in my career, I see IT moving from the back office to the front lines," says Esat. "It's great to have lean and streamlined processes, but the days of competing on the basis of efficiency are over. Most everyone has efficient processes now, so they're no longer a competitive advantage. It's not about the ERP system or the billing system or the order-to-cash system anymore. Those systems are important, but you can't compete on them."

In today's hyper-competitive markets, IT generates value by enabling business growth. That means the CIO has to be linked tightly to the business. The CIO must have excellent relationships with the CEO and the board of directors, and must be able to make the business case for investing in IT.

"The success of the business depends on the success of IT," says Esat. "Technology is the key enabling function. IT is tied to sales, marketing, distribution, supply chain—everything the business needs to be successful. So the CIO needs to understand the challenges of the business, understand the markets and how the business sells in those markets. The CIO needs to translate technology into business advantages that will differentiate the company from its competitors. CIOs who cannot do that will not be successful—and their companies will not be successful."

"The success of the business depends on the success of IT."

Esat advises CIOs to get out from behind the firewall and embrace the challenges of dealing with customers. "That's where the action is—out in front, with the customers," he says.

The four transformational technology trends of the current epoch—mobile, social, cloud, and big data—are all taking place in front of the firewall. These converging trends are driving a revolution in customer expectations. Today's customers not only want great products—they want great experiences.

Coca-Cola Enterprises is a great example of a company that uses IT to enable its business units to do a better job of interacting with customers—both online and offline. The company has issued mobile devices to 15,000 of its merchandisers to help them get the right mix of products to the right stores ahead of the competition. And the company uses its growing social media clout to launch large-scale marketing campaigns directly from social media platforms such as Facebook, where 25 million consumers have self-identified by "liking" its fan page.

The company also leverages its IT capabilities to get the most from its sponsorship of globally watched events such as the World Cup and the Olympics.

It helps that Esat reports directly to the company's CEO, John Brock. "That puts me at the table," says Esat. "There is no business plan that is not aligned with our technology capabilities. We don't have a separate IT plan—we have an integrated business plan. The integration starts at the top, with the relationship between the CEO and the CIO."

Sitting at the table is one thing—staying there is something else, says Esat. The CIO must work hard to develop and maintain strong connections to the C-suite and the board of directors. It's not just a matter of the CIO's survival—those relationships are also absolutely critical to the company's health and well-being.

"If the CIO does not have direct links to the CEO and the board, there is no way the company can gain value from the technology transformations taking place. The company will very quickly find itself in the hands of consultants. It will take longer and be more costly for the company to make the technology transformations it needs to be competitive," says Esat. "The CIO must be connected to the business in order to understand how technology can provide the greatest value and help the business achieve its goals. That's the biggest difference I see among CIOs—some want to be technology leaders and others want to be business leaders. But to succeed, you need to be both."

"The CIO must be connected to the business in order to understand how technology can provide the greatest value and help the business achieve its goals. That's the biggest difference I see among CIOs— some want to be technology leaders and others want to be business leaders. But to succeed, you need to be both."

Esat's close relationships with the company's senior management and board have enabled him to create what he describes as a "culture of experimentation." By continuously experimenting and adopting an array of newer technologies, the company has stayed ahead of the competition.

"We developed a mobility architecture in four months that allows us to communicate with our merchandisers and get products in the stores faster than our competitors. We couldn't have done it without the cloud," says Esat. "We've also moved all of our e-mail, our employee portals, and some of our development platform into the cloud. We use big data to get real-time feedback from our customers. We use social media to market our products to millions of consumers. We work closely with emerging technology vendors to experiment, learn, and innovate."

Some of these newer vendors could mature into future strategic partners, says Esat, joining traditional suppliers IBM and Microsoft in a new ecosystem of transformational IT providers.

When you chat with Esat, you can easily sense his passion and energy. He is a true believer in the transformational power of IT leadership.

Avon Calling

One of my favorite stories about using the cloud as a test bed for innovation was told to me by Donagh Herlihy, the SVP and CIO at Avon Products. Here is the background: Ranked 226 in the Fortune 500, Avon Products is the world's top direct seller of cosmetics and beauty-related items. I think it's fair to say that Avon's sales model is unique. Its independent sales force includes thousands of sales leaders, who in turn supervise the efforts of over 6 million sales representatives worldwide.

As you can imagine, moving real-time business information among this many people can be a challenge. In 2008, Avon decided that its global sales network needed a single, standardized information and reporting platform. Here's how Donagh describes the challenge:

> We knew that the new platform had to be action-oriented, provide immediate value, and be very easy to use. All representatives are independent entrepreneurs and many work part-time, so we couldn't have a system that required a massive training program. The system had to be simple, and it had to be fairly intuitive. It had to be Web-based, so people could use it on their home computers or smart phones.
>
> We wanted an application that would generate a "to-do list" for the sales leaders every morning . . . not a static list, but a list based on where they were in the sales cycle,

something that would show them which of their reps had not placed an order in that campaign, or had placed an order under the minimum threshold for generating a commission payment to the leader, who was late paying for an order . . . who was high potential and looked like they could (with the right encouragement and coaching) be promoted into leadership, who had attended a sales training event, and who had missed the event. We wanted to help them coach their reps more effectively and help them do a better job.

Avon studied the challenge diligently and considered several ways of moving forward. After careful consideration, the company narrowed the field of choices to three options. Here is Donagh's recollection of the decision-making process:

We looked at building the application ourselves and hosting it internally, which would have been the traditional Avon way.

We considered working with a traditional software vendor to develop the application. In that case, we could have hosted the application internally or had the vendor host the application.

We also looked at Salesforce.com, which was for us the unconventional choice at the time. It was also the least capital-intensive option.

Eventually, Avon chose Salesforce.com to develop the project. But capital avoidance was not the primary driver behind the company's decision to move into the cloud. Donagh explains:

Speed was the number one consideration. The economics were secondary. Going to the cloud meant we could begin testing the concept in weeks, without putting added stress on our IT organization or on our existing IT infrastructure. We could focus our energy and attention on the application itself, and that really narrowed the scope of the project.

Of course, it was also a very economical choice. But we made the decision based on speed to market. It was important to get the application up and running quickly.

In addition to speed and economy, there was a third consideration: We didn't have to overthink the project. Say, for example, that it hadn't worked in the test market. Then we would have said, "Okay, it's not working, this was a bad idea, let's stop and regroup." We could have done that, if necessary, because we hadn't invested in a lot of new infrastructure and software licenses, etc.

With the cloud model we were paying a fee per user per month, and if the application did not deliver we could fail quickly, stop the payments. We would have no investments to write off versus a traditional capital-intensive IT development.

The project was successful in its initial tests. The first pilot, in Eastern Europe, was fully developed and deployed in five months. The pilot was followed by successful deployments in markets in Western Europe and in Asia. As I'm writing these words, Avon has rolled out the application to over 25 markets and counting.

"By using a cloud model, we didn't have to worry about scalability, usage patterns, capacity planning, monitoring, or provisioning infrastructure. We inherently got the economics of a shared tenancy model."

Fine-tuning the application and focusing on the data to meet local business requirements and global operating standards was crucial to the success of the project. Avon didn't have to spend lots of time worrying about the project's infrastructure because the infrastructure was in the cloud.

By using a cloud model, we didn't have to worry about scalability, usage patterns, capacity planning, monitoring, or provisioning infrastructure. We inherently got the economics of a shared tenancy model.

As a consequence, Avon could focus on refining the details that were critical to its sales network. Focusing on those details contributed to the system's overall usability, which led to rapid adoption and usage by the sales leaders.

In retrospect, says Donagh, it seems inevitable that the cloud was the proper choice. But at the time Avon made its decision, the choice wasn't so obvious. After weighing the pros and cons, Avon bet on the cloud—and the bet paid off. The application drives sales revenues in the countries where it is used, due to the increased productivity of the sales leaders and their downline teams. In Donagh's own words, "It's a phenomenal payback, a game changer."

When the Model Fits

Dave Smoley is SVP and CIO at Flextronics, a Fortune Global 500 design, manufacture, distribution, and after-market services company. Based in Singapore, Flextronics operates in 30 countries—it is truly a global enterprise.

Complexity can become a challenge for large companies. Smart companies strive for speed and simplicity whenever possible. That's one of the reasons that Dave feels comfortable using cloud technology—it fits nicely with the company's strategic model.

"We're all about keeping it simple," says Dave. "In a cloud model, the provider is responsible for development, configuration, and support. The traditional model requires a much larger IT organization because you need administrators, project managers, business analysts, and other people to support the software and hardware."

> **"Today, the cloud can provide turnkey services and capabilities. You don't have to buy servers. You don't have to care whether an application is running on Java or Visual Basic. You can use any printer or any browser. The cloud simplifies IT. You could even say that it commoditizes IT."**

With four SaaS implementations under his belt, Dave is a cloud veteran. I asked him to describe the company's decision to adopt Workday as its HR solution. Here's a summary of what he told me:

IT is inherently complex. You need hardware, operating systems, drivers, utilities, applications, databases, and networks. Thirty years ago, you wrote your own programs in low-level assembly languages. Over time, the technology became more abstract, more high level, and more integrated. It's been an evolution.

Today, the cloud can provide turnkey services and capabilities. You don't have to buy servers. You don't have to care whether an application is running on Java or Visual Basic. You can use any printer or any browser. The cloud simplifies IT. You could even say that it commoditizes IT.

In IT, our job is solving business problems. Today, we will look first to a cloud solution, second to a traditional solution, and third to a custom-developed application. We will look at all three, but the underlying assumption is that the cloud is the first choice. When someone on my team sends me a recommendation, I expect to see two or three cloud offerings identified in the analysis.

Part of our decision to use Workday was based on my conviction that it was the right thing to do. And part of the decision was based on our corporate culture. As a tech company, we are more open to taking risks. We are also more aligned with the basic value proposition of the cloud—speed, simplicity, and lower costs. So I felt confident about pushing the envelope.

We estimated that using a cloud solution would result in a 30 to 50 percent reduction in total cost of ownership, compared to a package solution from a traditional vendor. On top of that, we looked at usability, and Workday was much more usable than the traditional solutions. Because it was less complex than a traditional solution, we would need fewer IT people in IT and HR to support it.

It also helped that Workday was located down the road from us. Our CEO, Mike McNamara, and I met on a Saturday morning with Workday's co-founders, Dave Duffield and Aneel Bhusri. They are very credible, trustworthy, and sincere guys. Their reputations are impeccable. We came out of the meeting and said, "These are the kind of people you want to be in business with."

Here's something else: If we had delegated this decision to a committee, it never would have happened. It would've been killed, because Workday is a small company and the IT team is used to dealing with big companies. A committee would have considered this too risky.

We implemented Workday almost completely on our own. In the first year, we had some help from the Workday team. We didn't depend on third-party integration partners. We did most of the implementation by ourselves.

And the result was a savings in the range of 30 percent. We took 80 HR systems and replaced them with one system. I consider it one of the premier accomplishments of my career.

I love this story because it captures so many aspects of the new cloud model—the speed, the simplicity, and the reduced costs. I included a version of this story in my first book, *The Transformational CIO*, and I really wanted to re-examine it from a cloud perspective in this book. I'm delighted that Dave had the time to retell the story and add more significant details. Thank you, Dave.

Chapter 8

The New Speed of Change

On May 23, 2011, Toyota Motor Corporation (TMC) and Salesforce.com announced a strategic alliance to build "Toyota Friend," a private social network for Toyota customers and their cars. Toyota President Akio Toyoda offered this observation: "Social networking services are transforming human interaction and modes of communication. The automobile needs to evolve in step with that transformation. I am always calling for Toyota to make ever-better cars. The alliance that we announce today is an important step forward in achieving that goal."

By coincidence, I had scheduled a telephone interview with Barbra Cooper, group VP and CIO at Toyota North America, for the next day. Sometimes, you just get lucky!

In her current role at Toyota, Barbra is responsible for the strategy, development, and operation of all systems and technology that support Toyota in the North America region. Cooper also heads the University of Toyota, located in Torrance, California, which provides training and education for Toyota associates, as well as Toyota and Lexus dealerships and distributors globally.

She is also part of the leadership team that develops and nurtures innovative projects such as Toyota Friend. Here's some background information from the company:

Toyota Friend will be powered by Salesforce Chatter, a private social network used by businesses, and will be offered, first in Japan, initially with Toyota's electric vehicles (EV) and plug-in hybrid vehicles (PHV) due in 2012.

Toyota Friend will be a private social network that connects Toyota customers with their cars, their dealership, and with Toyota. Toyota Friend will provide a variety of product and service information as well as essential maintenance tips, creating a rich car ownership experience. For example, if an EV or PHV is running low on battery power, Toyota Friend would notify the driver to recharge in the form of a "tweet"-like alert. In addition, while Toyota Friend will be a private social network, customers can choose to extend their communication to family, friends, and others through public social networks such as Twitter and Facebook. The service will also be accessible through smart phones, tablet PCs, and other advanced mobile devices.

To date, TMC has developed its own telematics services to connect people, cars, and their surroundings. Through Toyota Friend, TMC aims to offer its telematics services worldwide. Moving forward, TMC plans to advance toward the realization of future mobility by teaming up proactively with global IT companies.

Although TMC and Salesforce.com will launch their partnership with the building of Toyota Friend, in the future the companies plan to develop cloud services for TMC's open platform and create new business opportunities leveraging their respective strengths.

Salesforce.com and TMC will each make investments in Toyota Media Service Co. (TMS), which oversees TMC's global cloud platform development. Salesforce.com will invest 223 million yen and TMC will invest 442 million yen. Microsoft Corporation, which on April 6 (2011) announced a strategic partnership with TMC to build a global platform for next-generation telematics services, will invest 335 million yen.

If you needed an example to illustrate how big companies are leveraging the convergence of cloud, mobile, and social computing technologies to create new business opportunities, this is it.

And it's not a bunch of marketing hype. Alliances such as this one represent more than just business as usual—they are the future of business.

And that's one of the reasons I was delighted to interview Barbra the day after Toyota and Salesforce.com made their announcement. The timing was perfect.

In many ways, Barbra is an archetype for the modern transformational CIO. She has an impressive resume and a long list of accomplishments. In 1996, McGraw-Hill Publishing named her as one of the Top 100 Women in Computing. *Computerworld* listed her among the Premier IT Leaders in 2001. She received a *CIO* 100 Award in 2005 from *CIO* magazine. Ziff Davis's *CIO Insight* magazine ranked her sixth of the top 100 global CIOs in 2007, and *CIO* magazine's Executive Council awarded her the Distinguished Member Award for Most

Valuable Content. In the same year, she was inducted into the
CIO Hall of Fame.

But she doesn't spend a lot of time looking in the rearview
mirror. Like a winning race car driver, she's already looking
ahead to the next series of turns on the track.

In our conversation, Barbra compared the current cycle of
transformational change with the previous cycle. Here is a
summary of what she said:

*I've watched several big cycles of change and transformation.
The cycle we're experiencing today reminds me of the cycle
that occurred when the PC was introduced in the workplace.
That first wave of personalized technology had a profound
impact on the corporate business model.*

*Although the changes were dramatic, they occurred rela-
tively slowly. The software evolved over years, and it was still
tethered in many ways to the old world of green screens and
batch processing. Today, change happens much more quickly.*

*I think the biggest difference between then and now is that
today's end user is far more independent. The newer technology offers them much more personalization and indepen-
dence. When you combine that with the very rapid product
development cycles of various technologies, it raises some
very serious issues about how we manage IT and how we
adapt to change.*

*My generation of IT leadership was all about control.
Fundamentally, our goals were achieving reliability and pre-
dictability. So we created limits and standards that enabled us
to manage the reliability of complex systems and keep the costs
of those systems under control.*

Much of that has flipped over the years. You don't have so much control as you had in the past. And you can't manhandle the workforce like you could in the past. You can't tell a new employee they have to work here 10 years before we'll give you a BlackBerry.

The old tricks won't work in today's environment. The millennials entering the workforce have been consuming technology for quite a while. They've watched industries adapt to the needs of the modern consumer. They are much better informed than their predecessors. They want to custom design their own jeans and configure their own cars. How can you tell them they can't have something when they can get whatever they want through the back door in 10 minutes?

That's the biggest challenge I see coming for IT leaders today. And while it might sound like a governance issue or a policy issue, it's fundamentally deeper.

The root of the problem is data, says Barbra. All of our technologies—devices, systems, networks—generate a fantastic amount of data. The modern world runs on data, and there's a growing awareness that data is valuable.

> **"The old tricks won't work in today's environment. The millennials entering the workforce have been consuming technology for quite a while. They've watched industries adapt to the needs of the modern consumer. They are much better informed than their predecessors. They want to custom design their own jeans and configure their own cars. How can you tell them they can't have something when they can get whatever they want through the back door in 10 minutes?"**

Data are a by-product of every product and service we provide or consume. The data explosion is profoundly altering the way we look at all aspects of modern business. The impact of all this on the CIO is inescapable.

In the past, CIOs were primarily valued for their ability to provision service. A good CIO interpreted the needs of the business and provided the technology required to meet those needs. IT was (and in some organizations still is) seen as a utility, not much different from electricity or running water.

But in an information economy—an economy in which the data surrounding a product or service are perceived as being more potentially valuable than the product or service itself—the CIO's role is very different.

In a globalized information economy, the CIO's role is (or should be) less about provisioning IT services and more about providing information that can be used by the enterprise to create value through innovation.

Here's the net takeaway: In the old days, the CIO drove value through efficiency. Today, the CIO drives value through innovation. This trend is especially visible in the automotive industry, as Barbra notes:

This market has leveled out in many ways. The niches have pretty much been filled. There's a finite number of ways you can bend metal. Most cars are basically similar. How do you get an edge or a competitive advantage in the market? We have to differentiate ourselves in new ways.

We're trying to see the car from the perspective of consumers who are text messaging and communicating with their friends and family through social media. We're figuring out how to get into that space and customize the experience for our customers. We're doing it their way, as opposed to just saying, "Okay, here's the car, get in."

And that's why we're working with suppliers like Salesforce. com and Microsoft in alliances that look more like joint ventures than traditional vendor/customer relationships. We're innovating from all sides, instead of saying, "Here's what we want, now go do it for us."

I find it absolutely fascinating how the innovation process mirrors the market. The alliances described by Barbra reflect the realities of today's consumer-driven markets.

Modern markets, to varying degrees, are self-organizing. Because modern markets change so quickly—too quickly, according to some—traditional command-and-control structures just get in the way.

This general rule applies to all kinds of organizations. When things change very slowly (like during the Middle Ages), an inflexible, top-down hierarchy will get the job done. When things change extremely rapidly, organizing structures must be flat and flexible, or they will be overrun.

Updating the Mental Model

During my conversation with Barbra, we spoke about the differences among past, present, and future generations of IT leaders. Many of the CIOs we know earned their stripes by overseeing the implementation of large-scale ERP systems. Those "once in a lifetime" projects were truly transformational, and they permanently changed the landscape of IT.

The Herculean struggles over ERP have largely subsided. You rarely hear debates or arguments over ERP any more. Once considered revolutionary, ERP is now the norm in large companies. The next generation of CIOs won't spend their days and nights worrying about ERP—they'll have other fish to fry.

There's an old saying that generals always try to fight the last war. I suppose that it's human nature to take comfort in the familiar. We're all creatures of habit, and deep down, we hate change.

But the world has changed, and there's a limit to what we can learn from history. Making the most of newer technologies such as cloud, social, and mobile computing will require new leadership strategies. More pointedly, perhaps, it will require a new way of looking at the relationship between IT and the enterprise. Here is what Barbra told me:

IT is being increasingly disintermediated. Within the next couple of years, the business will be able go out and directly source almost any IT service that it needs. We're not talking here about one or two rogue business units going around IT. We're talking about the whole corporation—all of your internal customers, and all of their customers.

The pressure to change is coming from all sides. The old CIO mental model is not sustainable. I know people who are just digging in deeper, putting up fences, and hoping for the best. But that won't work. We need a new mental model for the CIO. We need to develop that new model, and then we need to build to it—aggressively.

Defining the new model, fleshing it out, making it real, and putting it to work won't be easy. This is a pivotal moment for CIOs. Transforming IT from its current state to its future state will require making a break with the past. It will take original thinking and genuine leadership to create the next generation of IT, but it needs to be done.

Failing to commit the time, energy, and resources necessary to build a new IT model would be irresponsible. I think it's fair to say that if the CIO doesn't step up and take the primary leadership role in building the new model, someone else will.

I think it's important to emphasize the need for reexamining past practices and old strategies. Toyota, which built its business on quality control and continuous process improvement, is now focusing more of its energy and resources on innovating for its customers. That is a sharp break from the past, in which innovation was usually reserved for improving internal processes and reducing costs.

Kaizen is the name for this philosophy of continuous process improvement. No company embodied the spirit of *kaizen* more than Toyota. But as one top auto executive recently said, "You can't *kaizen* your way into the competitive global marketplace."

In a continuously changing economy, efficiency can only take you so far. Now is the time for innovation. That much seems clear.

But let's do a quick reality check: Most CIOs still focus primarily on efficiency, consistency, and reliability. Innovation scares them. Innovation is hard to predict and difficult to control. If you see your primary role as being the person in charge of making sure that everything runs smoothly, innovation can look a lot like the enemy. And that's the problem.

Frankly, I don't see anything wrong with looking at innovation as a problem. As we all know, every problem can be managed. That means that you can manage innovation.

At the risk of stating the obvious, you will need some kind of process for managing innovation properly. You will need to invent the process and customize it for your own company. The best way to start is by forming an innovation process committee. I suggest recruiting members of your IT leadership team to form the nucleus of the committee. Here are some questions for them to consider at the committee's first meeting:

1. How do we move from an efficiency mind-set to an innovation mind-set?

2. How do we shift the organization's focus from improving internal processes to putting smiles on the faces of external customers?

3. How do we learn to embrace change instead of fearing it?

4. How do we encourage people to innovate, and how do we reward them when the company benefits from their innovations?

We'll return to the theme of putting process around innovation in following chapters. Right now, I would like to share another story that Barbra told me during our conversation.

Innovation under Pressure

In 2008, Toyota Motor Corporation passed General Motors to become the world's Number 1 carmaker. It was an amazing victory for Toyota, and it vindicated the company's long-standing commitment to technical excellence and continuous improvement.

But things went downhill quickly. Global sales plunged, and the company recorded the largest losses in its history. Toyota returned to profitability by the end of 2009, only to face another crisis: a series of recalls that damaged the brand's reputation. Toyota became the focus of government investigations and court actions. James E. Lentz, president and chief operating officer of Toyota Motor Sales (TMS) USA, was called to testify before Congress.

With the company's reputation and financial health at stake, it became imperative for Toyota to provide accurate information that would set the record straight and counter the groundswell of negative sentiment. But finding and surfacing information in a timely manner was not an easy task. The information wasn't stored in one central repository; it was in different systems in various parts of the world. Much of the information was actually unstructured data, which meant that it would be difficult to analyze.

Barbra realized that the company would have to act quickly and decisively to get ahead of the mounting criticism. Here's the story in her words:

> It was real obvious to me that we didn't have information that was timely enough to be effective. When you wade into the world of data, you're dealing with data warehouses, data marts, complex analytics—all of this very complicated and cryptic stuff that only a handful of people know how to use.
>
> In the midst of the most challenging demands of this crisis, I took the risk of acquiring a database tool from Endeca that would allow us to locate and analyze both structured and unstructured data regarding the claims being made about our products and very quickly gain new insights that were impossible before. After we had the ability to see the data, we could be more proactive and more confident. It was a huge boost for us.

The new data software also demonstrated that IT could innovate successfully, even under the most intense pressure. But the story doesn't end there. The system has been formalized and is now used to analyze complex data from various sources, including customer call centers and warranty databases.

> The nice thing about this software is that it slices and crawls across any kind of data we think might be possibly relevant. We've created templates for examining complex data from internal and external source. We've given our quality teams a

better structure for looking at data. You don't need elaborate syntax queries and that sort of stuff. You don't need to be a computer programmer to look at the data and run analytics.

Now we can look at data and ask ourselves, "Okay, how do we act on this data?" Not only have we reduced the time it takes to get information, we've changed the way we think about data. That's a big change.

One of the most remarkable lessons from this story is that CIOs really can change the business for the better. It takes intelligence, leadership, and courage—but it can be done. Barbra frames it this way:

In a crisis or in a competitive situation, you've got to be able to do those types of things. When you're the CIO, you've got to step up and be innovative. If you can't—if all you can do is worry about your metrics and your servers and delivering your projects on time—you will be disintermediated. The business will go out and use a credit card to buy the IT services it needs, and they'll only call you when there's a problem.

The Cloud on Wheels

I didn't want to leave Barbra without revisiting the topic of cloud computing and Toyota's new venture with Salesforce. com. When I asked her for more details of the project, she agreed to speak only in general terms:

Suffice it to say that we're placing a big bet on these technologies. We're looking at the car as an extension of the consumer's lifestyle, which involves mobile and social computing. This is the beginning of a complete integration of consumers and their vehicles, at multiple levels. Social media is just one aspect of it. The younger generation sees cars very differently. Cars are more than just transportation. In Japan, people also use their cars to generate electric power for their homes. We're heading toward cars that are much more intelligent, much more efficient, and much more integrated with our lifestyles.

Ten years ago, we didn't have the technology to take this vision and run with it. Now we have the technology, and we also have relationships with vendors and suppliers who share the vision and who understand that we're all innovating together.

Campaigning in the Cloud

We visited briefly with Tom Peck in Part I of this book. Tom is the CIO of Levi Strauss, a company that has been a leader in innovation for more than 150 years. I asked him to talk in greater detail about the company's cloud-based initiatives, and here's what he told me:

First, let's align on the definition—cloud computing is a deployment model for IT solutions accessed over the Internet. This model is in contrast to traditional IT deployments using on-premise solutions managed in-house. Cloud computing differs from earlier models of managed services as the cloud infrastructure scales up and down as your workload expands and contracts, and you typically only pay for what you use. However, cloud computing is increasingly used in the broader sense to refer to any type of managed IT service which enables faster deployment while minimizing upfront costs.

We have been using SaaS or hosted solutions for many years. What is new to us is PaaS, IaaS, and leveraging the cloud for pay-as-you-go, on-demand scalability. In the past year we have heavily leveraged the cloud for our online sites including marketing and promotions, consumer games and give aways, external blogs and more—for anything where we expect significant increases in short-term volume where we lack the scale and/or capabilities internally.

Just as one example, we used the cloud for our Dockers® Super Bowl campaign. To reinvigorate the khaki brand, we launched the Dockers® "Wear the Pants" marketing campaign in 2010. The NFL® Super Bowl marketing campaign served as the traditional broadcast media platform, driving unprecedented levels of online traffic through an integrated Web, social, and mobile solution using cloud technology and CRM.

Challenges: It was actually so successful that even the cloud didn't scale fast and big enough. In a cloud, you need to be careful that you don't limit the scale to what you pay for.

Working with multiple partners across an ecosystem in both testing/prep as well as when problems occur was also a challenge. The end-state technology solution involved 13 vendors and agencies working across seven different Levi Strauss teams ranging from marketing through IT. Where is the smoking gun when something goes wrong?

Result: It was a huge consumer success that we could not have done in-house. A few highlights: 4,000 page views per second on the Web and 200 hits per second on mobile devices; unprecedented sustained levels of traffic to dockers.com; we were the number 1 and number 2 most searched item on Google during and after the game; it received 4.2 out of 5 stars on YouTube; Nielsen BuzzMetrics reporting that in comparison to other Super Bowl advertisers, Dockers® had the biggest surge in Facebook® fans and Twitter® followers; and much more.

We've also tested our ERP in an appliance-based cloud offering. Challenges: getting the software partner to "certify"

*that it will work in the cloud and dealing with multiple ven-
dors in the offering. Result: We proved out the capability but
now we're waiting for that "life event" (i.e., server refresh cycle, new project, etc.) to spur the purchase.*

*Additionally, we have put some of our test and development
environments in virtualized, cloud environments. We are in
the process of putting e-mail in the cloud. Challenges: It wasn't
plug-n-play as we were sold. Result: Painfully worked through
it but now going live.*

*As discussed earlier, the consumerization of IT is creating a
value gap that could disrupt traditional IT service providers.
Cloud computing is a reinforcing trend. IT solutions lagging
behind user requirements force users to take matters into their
own hands, leveraging consumer technologies and the Internet. Doing so will reduce users' dependence on traditional
technology sources. Don't fight change. Don't fight the cloud.
Figure out how to embrace it.*

> **"Don't fight change. Don't fight the cloud. Figure out
> how to embrace it."**

I also asked Tom to talk about the factors that influenced
the decision to choose a cloud-based service, and what kind
of benefits he expected to realize from the cloud. I found his
response candid and illuminating:

*As far as the merits that influence our decision to choose a
cloud-based service, I want speed of deployment, the ability to
surge or scale on demand and the ability to rapidly build and
change components such as test environments for software.
It's also great for when I lack the internal expertise. I must*

admit that I am still a slight cynic in regards to the cloud. While there are many merits, there are an equal number of challenges. Until I can get my ERP in the cloud, my business intelligence (BI) in the cloud, help close an acquisition faster via the cloud, and help the business open new stores or enter new markets, we can't just assume the cloud will solve all our problems.

A business executive once tore out a newspaper clipping about how the "cloud" will reduce costs, speed implementation, and allow him to reduce his IT staff and costs. I had to explain to him that there is a lot of truth to that; however, it's not a blanket assumption. In this case, we had to separate out sales and marketing hype from the practical reality that not everything is in the cloud. At least not yet, anyway.

I also asked Tom to describe how technology has changed the way Levi Strauss responds to the market:

There have been many changes, but perhaps the most impactful is social shopping. Last year Levi's® and Facebook® broke new ground as we were the first retail company to integrate Facebook's® social plug-in "like" button with our Levi's® e-commerce site. In addition, we launched the Levi's® Friends Store, the first social online shopping experience. Using Facebook's® Graph APIs, we built an entire social commerce experience as an extension of our e-Commerce site. We created a new customized social shopping experience that has changed the way people shop online—and made buying jeans online more fun.

We took product reviews one step further by giving people the opportunity to see what their friends "like" and what products their friends are buying. This allows our passionate ambassadors to find and share information about their favorite Levi's®

products. Upon launch, we saw significant increases in traffic coming to levi.com from our Facebook® page.

Our number of Levi's® Facebook® fans has increased from 180,000 to over 4 million in less than a year. And we use our Levi's® brand leveraged Facebook® to amplify other events such as concerts and promotions. Our partnership with Facebook® continues as we leverage the success of this initiative to drive continued investments in social media.

"Newer technologies have the risk of making CIOs obsolete if they don't understand how to harness the power of them."

I also posed this very general question to Tom: How would you describe the impact of newer technologies (such as cloud, mobile, and social computing) on the role of the CIO in a modern organization? Can you cite some specific examples of a newer technology that has had an impact on your organization?

As stated earlier, the role of today's CIO is as much about staying apprised of and leveraging consumer technologies as it is about building and buying enterprise applications. Newer technologies have the risk of making CIOs obsolete if they don't understand how to harness the power of them. End users see consumer applications that allow them to put music and photos in the cloud for collaborative sharing on demand. Why can't those same consumers, acting now as employees, see our company's product catalogs digitally on demand while on sales calls? We must stay apprised and informed.

Part III

Building Value

"Cloud computing is not the savior of IT. It is nothing but a way to deploy your enterprise architecture in a way that has the potential to be more productive and cost effective. In essence, it is a tool, not a way of life."

—David S. Linthicum
*Cloud Computing and SOA Convergence
in Your Enterprise*

Chapter 9

Pushing the Envelope

Where do we enter the cloud? What's the best way for my company to get started? How do I decide which service to move into the cloud first?

If you had posed these questions to a roomful of CIOs two years ago, most of them would have recommended starting with corporate e-mail. If you ask the same questions today, you are likely to hear a range of answers. And the answers would be more nuanced. Many of the answers would start with these words: *It depends* . . .

It depends on the size of your company. It depends on the level of regulation in your industry. It depends on the needs of the market. It depends on whether you manufacture products or provide services. It depends on whether your company is privately owned or publicly owned.

Obviously, there are lots of variables. But as I interviewed more CIOs, some certainties arose. Every CIO said they would make sure there was a strong business case for moving a service or capability into the cloud. Nobody said they would move into the cloud just for the sake of being in the cloud.

So I found a sense of unanimity around the idea that you have to make the business case for moving into the cloud. I remember thinking, *that's a good sign*. But I remember noticing that only a handful of CIOs had fleshed out a real process for making decisions about the cloud.

> **"We didn't focus on the vocabulary of the cloud. We focused instead on using the cloud to give us the flexibility and agility to respond to changes facing the business."**

That's why I was especially glad to interview Steve Phillpott, the CIO of Amylin Pharmaceuticals. Steve is a graduate of the U.S. Naval Academy, and he spent several years as a naval aviator, flying jets from aircraft carriers. Like pilots everywhere, Steve is extremely careful. But once he's determined the risks and figured out the best course of action, he moves quickly and decisively. He can "push the envelope" when necessary, but only because he knows where the edge of the envelope is. Here is Steve's account of his company's "journey" into the cloud:

We've been on this journey for quite some time. We saw the cloud coming in 2008. At that time, lots of people were getting stuck around cloud terminology. They said, "What does all of this really mean?" And then, in late 2010 and early 2011, they said, "Okay, we get the concept, but where do we start?"

We took a completely different approach. We didn't focus on the vocabulary of the cloud. We focused instead on using the cloud to give us the flexibility and agility to respond to changes facing the business.

I think it's illuminating that Steve focuses first on the needs of the business. If there's a "secret formula" for successful cloud deployments, that's it: Keep your eyes on what the business needs.

Steve's approach to developing a cloud strategy was influenced by *The New Age of Innovation: Driving Co-Created Value through Global Networks* by C. K. Prahalad and M. S. Krishnan. In the book, the authors present two simple statements to summarize their worldview:

$$N = 1$$

$$R = G$$

The first statement, $N = 1$, refers to the concept of the customer (a segment of one) and the business collaborating to produce products, services, and experiences that benefit both the customer and the business. The concept builds on the ideas of mass customization and one-to-one marketing, and envisions a radically new relationship between the customer and the business.

The second statement, $R = G$, is easier to understand. It simply means that resources are global. The implications of this apparently simple statement are profound, and they are absolutely critical to the formation of a practical cloud strategy. $R = G$ implies that no company can possibly own all

the resources required to respond meaningfully and successfully to the needs of its customers.

If you accept R = G as true, then the cloud makes a lot of
sense from a business perspective. Since it's impossible for
any company to possess all the resources it needs to satisfy
its customers, companies *must* have practical strategies
for reaching beyond their traditional boundaries to obtain the
resources they need to stay in business. Clearly, the cloud
represents one way for companies to reach outside themselves for resources that would be impractical or impossible
for them to own or acquire.

And that's the reason you need a cloud strategy—not
because the cloud is cool technology, but because the
business needs it to remain competitive in a global economy.

Several years ago, you could have argued that all of this is
merely theory. It would be difficult to make that argument
today. The modern economy isn't just global—it's consumer-
driven. Consumerization is everywhere, and it's one of the
factors driving newer technologies such as the cloud.

Steve knew in his gut that the cloud would be part of the
solution for dealing with the realities of R = G. But he needed
a robust and repeatable process for figuring out which services and capabilities to move into the cloud. So here is what
Steve did:

*Back in 2008, we went through our entire IT budget and
rebuilt it as a list of services. We didn't say, "This is how much*

*we spend on hardware, software, maintenance, and staff."
Instead we said, "This is how much we spend providing each
service." We had a list of 80 to 100 services that we provided,
and that became our IT budget.*

*Then I ranked the services in terms of cost, with the most
expensive on top. Then I could immediately see which services
were costing the most. Some of the more expensive services had
to stay in-house for competitive or regulatory reasons. Not everything is an appropriate use case for the cloud delivery model.*

*But in some cases, we had expensive services that weren't
providing a competitive advantage and weren't subject to regulation. Those became the first candidates for outsourcing or
moving to the cloud.*

Rebuilding the IT budget and calculating the real cost of
the services IT provided to the business was not an easy task.
It required months of hard work. But Steve knew that it had to
be done. "Now I can do an apples-to-apples comparison
between what we're spending to provide a service and what
it would cost if we outsourced it or used a cloud/software-as-
a-service (SaaS) provider," says Steve.

> **"But in some cases, we had expensive services that
> weren't providing a competitive advantage and
> weren't subject to regulation. Those became the first
> candidates for outsourcing or moving to the cloud."**

There were other advantages to Steve's approach. The new
"cost-by-services" budget model also creates opportunities to
break down the invisible silos that tend to emerge within IT

departments as roles become more specialized. Emphasizing the cost of services over the cost of applications makes it easier to get people focused on what's important. Here is Steve's take on the danger of letting the silos remain standing:

In IT, we often get too focused on the application. Someone might say, for instance, "I'm a Siebel person" because that's the application they know. But when you look at IT from a cost-by-services perspective, you can say, "No, you are not a Siebel person, you are a person who understands customer relationship data and customer relationship management systems." So the focus is no longer on the application, the focus is on the skill set you need to provide the service.

As we all know, silos can form in any department, and they often create a sense of inertia that is hard to overcome. When silos are removed, departments usually become more efficient and more open to innovation.

One of the innovations Steve introduced was a cloud solution for the company's human resources information system (HRIS). Here's the story in Steve's own words:

We had an on-premise HRIS that had taken four years and several million to build. After making that kind of investment, there was naturally some resistance to moving to another system. But we made the case for going with a cloud-based solution from Workday, and it's making a huge difference. The project was deployed in months, not years. I've done two major upgrades of the system in the past six months with zero capital spend. Most important, it frees up time and resources so we can focus on bringing innovation to the business.

I like that story because it illustrates the value of bringing a practical mind-set to the cloud. It made sense to "outsource" the HRIS to the cloud, so that's what the company did. The decision was based on a careful "apples-to-apples" analysis of the costs and functionality. In another situation, when Steve's team agreed that it was no longer practical to maintain an on-premise data center, they chose a different route.

After considering several alternatives, the team decided to migrate the company's data center applications to a much larger data center owned by a specialized provider in Phoenix. Steve lightheartedly refers to the migration project as "data center as a service," but it's not a cloud solution, and technically, it's not even outsourcing. Steve explains:

Basically, we have a dedicated area within a huge data center that's the size of seven football fields. We still own the applications, we own the racks, and we own the equipment. They own the building. They make sure the network capacity is there. They provide air conditioning and cooling. Our power savings alone make it worth the effort. It fit our R = G strategy, as this is their core competency. They are continually focused on efficiency and can manage a data center much better than I would ever be able to.

"Some people are still struggling with the question of where to get started. I tell them that the opportunity cost of procrastination just continues to climb."

This is an incredibly creative approach to a common problem. For most companies, the data centers provide little competitive advantage. So they might seem like perfect candidates for outsourcing or migrating to the cloud. But if you're in regulated industries like pharma, health care, or financial services, your options are restricted. So you have to be creative. I'll let Steve have the last words on this subject:

> One size doesn't fit all. We have to be flexible enough to innovate, and we can't get trapped in one box. We want a very, very broad range of capabilities because we don't know exactly what the business is going to ask from us in the future. What we do know is that resources will transcend the traditional boundaries of the corporation. What we need isn't necessarily going to be found within our own four walls.
>
> The cloud isn't the answer to everything. But there will definitely be opportunities to leverage the cloud delivery model, and part of the job is finding those opportunities.
>
> Some people are still struggling with the question of where to get started. I tell them that the opportunity cost of procrastination just continues to climb.

Two Sides of the Same Coin

My friend John Hill, the former Siemens CTO, says it's important to remember that every cloud implementation contains two essential elements. One element is the technology and the other element is the business model. These two elements are complementary and fundamental. You can't have one without the other. They are two sides of the same coin.

Let's look at the business side first. It should be provisioned through some kind of self-service portal so consumers can access it easily and usage can be measured. It should be on demand and easily activated. It should be a service, not a capital product. It should be "pay by the drink" so you can stop buying when you've had enough.

Provisioning should be policy-driven, highly automated, and immediate. If you have to wait a week, it's not the cloud. If it requires a long-term contract, it's not the cloud.

On the technology side, it should be accessible through standard Internet protocols—if you need to install software, it's not a cloud service. It should be dynamically scalable and elastic, which means that when demand goes up, consumption rises along with it.

> **"The cloud is technology married to a business model."**

It doesn't have to be virtual, but it is often enabled by virtualization. As mentioned, provisioning must be immediate and highly automated—ideally through a self-service portal. If it's the cloud, it probably will be multitenant, meaning that multiple consumers will use it at the same time.

"The cloud is technology married to a business model," says John. "If you don't have that marriage of technology and business, then you don't have a cloud. Vendors who are just selling hardware are not selling cloud. Vendors who are just selling software are not selling cloud."

Of course, we're speaking in generalities here. There are no absolutes at this stage of the game. The cloud—as a technology and as a business model—is still young, and the rules have yet to be written. We're all pioneers, and we're all likely to make a few wrong turns. We might even stumble, but that's why we want to step forward deliberately. It's okay to be cautious, as long as our caution doesn't prevent us from taking action.

And of course, it all depends on your perspective. Following is a quick table sorting out several key differences between the technology perspective and the business perspective on cloud computing:

Technology	Business
Rapid access through standard Internet protocols	Self-service
Automation orchestration	Pay by the drink
Dynamically scalable/Elastic	Operating expense (OPEX), not capital expense (CAPEX)
Multi-tenant	Immediate provisioning
Anywhere, everywhere, all the time availability	Easy on/off
	Policy-driven

Now that we've defined the cloud as a combination of technology *and* business, let's talk about the value it offers. IBM recently published a list of cloud benefits:

- Driving business innovation with a large number of new applications developed with newly affordable cloud development environments.

- Increasing business responsiveness.

- Lower total cost of ownership and improving asset utilization.

- Providing an open and elastic IT environment.

- Optimizing IT investments.

- Enabling real-time data streams and information sharing.

- Providing globally available resources.

The list is by no means exhaustive, but it serves as a good starting point for looking at the cloud as a value driver. Earlier in the book, we've seen examples of CIOs using the cloud to enable innovation and support business growth. And I've been hammering at the idea that modern CIOs should focus more on top-line revenue growth and worry less about striving relentlessly for greater efficiency. That being said, the cloud also offers some serious opportunities for reducing IT operating and capital costs. Because of its very nature, the cloud will make it easier for many people to use available IT resources, and as we all know, increased utilization decreases IT costs.

Because the cloud enables rapid provisioning on a pay-by-the-drink basis, IT should be able to reduce the cost of capital investment. Imagine not having to build systems to handle peak usage—that's the promise of cloud computing.

When IBM Research compared the costs of application testing services in a private cloud versus a traditional testing environment, it saw hardware savings of 65 percent (from reduced infrastructure and improved hardware utilization); software savings of 27 percent (from lower licensing costs resulting from improved utilization); system administration savings of 45 percent (from lower administration and operating costs); and provisioning savings of 76 percent (from lower labor costs in service request management).

These are impressive numbers, and they make a pretty good case for including a cloud option as a matter of routine when considering any new or additional services or capabilities.

A Multiplicity of Clouds

When I was learning how to sail, I became aware of just how many different types of clouds there are in the sky—stratus, cumulus, cumulonimbus, cirrus, lenticular, cirrocumulus stratiformis, and dozens more. So I wasn't totally surprised to discover that there are lots of different kinds of computing clouds. Let's take a look at the various types and nomenclatures you will find when exploring the universe of cloud computing.

There are two general ways to look at the cloud, and it's important to understand the difference between them. We can look at the cloud from the perspective of *service,* and we can look at the cloud from the perspective of *deployment.*

Service

Let's begin with service. The three cloud service models that you are most likely familiar with are:

1. Software-as-a-service (SaaS).

2. Platform-as-a-service (PaaS).

3. Infrastructure-as-a-service (IaaS).

Here are extremely brief and very basic descriptions of each:

- SaaS enables you to "rent" finished applications that are running on a service provider's infrastructure. Providers include Google, Salesforce.com, Workday, Right Now Technologies, and many others.

- PaaS enables you to use a service provider's platform to develop and test your own applications and to deploy them over the Internet. Providers include Amazon Web Services (EC2), VMForce, NetSuite, Microsoft Azure, Clickability, LongJump, and others.

- IaaS enables you to "rent" a broader range of basic IT resources (e.g., storage, network, bandwidth, memory). Providers include Amazon Web Services, Rackspace, Flexiscale, Joyent, and others.

But as cloud expert David Linthicum notes, it doesn't end there. In addition to the "top three" service models, there are also storage-as-a-service, database-as-a-service, information-as-a-service, process-as-a-service, integration-as-a-service, security-as-a-service, governance-as-a-service, and testing-as-a-service.

As you can see from their names, each of these types of service offers specific benefits. For more detailed descriptions of these service components, I recommend reading David's excellent book, *Cloud Computing and SOA Convergence in Your Enterprise: A Step-by-Step Guide*.

Deployment

From the deployment perspective, there are four broad categories:

1. Public cloud.

2. Private cloud.

3. Hybrid cloud.

4. Community cloud.

The public cloud is the deployment model that tends to garner the most publicity. It is also the model that, quite frankly, you are least likely to use if you are responsible for developing an enterprise cloud strategy. The main problem with the public cloud is data security, and until that problem is solved, business users will regard it with understandable skepticism. That being said, it requires the least amount of investment—which means that it is probably the best place to being testing and exploring the cloud.

Large organizations are likely to see the private cloud model as the most logical choice. Security is less likely to be a problem in a private cloud for the simple reason that private clouds are—private. You own it and you decide who gets to use it. The other nice thing about the private cloud model is that large corporations already have much of the virtualization infrastructure required to make it work.

The advantage of the hybrid model is that it provides the best of both worlds—the security of the private cloud and the low cost of the public cloud. Large companies with highly variable demands for IT services can use the hybrid model to ensure that needs are met during peak periods. In a sense, the hybrid model leverages the public cloud as a "spillover" system.

The community cloud model takes into account that certain types of cloud computing are more likely to be used by specific industry verticals, and that it makes sense for companies within those verticals (such as financial services or health care) to use clouds that have been designed and architected to meet their needs more closely than generic clouds.

Following are three diagrams based on IBM's vision of a practical cloud ecosystem. These are high-level diagrams, not intended to serve as detailed blueprints for formal cloud architectures. They are useful references, however, and they can certainly help you get the cloud conversation started.

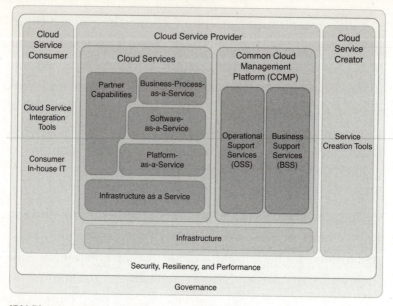

IBM Diagram of Cloud Reference Architecture
Source: IBM

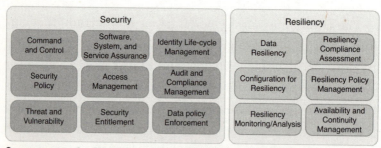

Components of a Cloud Security and Resiliency Architecture
Source: IBM

Turn of the Tide

I studied hundreds of surveys, reports, and white papers over the course of writing this book. One really stood out from the pack, and I want to share its findings with you.

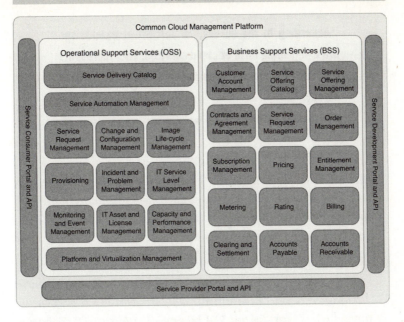

Components of a Common Cloud Management Platform
Source: IBM

Published in June 2011 by Avanade, its title is "Global Survey: Has Cloud Computing Matured?" Its content is based on a March 2011 survey of 573 C-level executives, business unit leaders, and IT decision makers in 18 countries.

Avanade, as many of you know, was launched as a joint venture in 2000 by Accenture and Microsoft. It provides technology services across multiple sectors including telecommunications, financial services, public sector, multinational retailing, manufacturing, and entertainment.

The report is the third in an annual series, and it reveals some interesting trends in the way technology executives look at the cloud. Here are some nuggets from the report:

"According to the survey, 74 percent of enterprises are using some form of cloud services. This represents a 25 percent growth since Avanade's September 2009 survey."

Looking to the year ahead, 55 percent of companies report their IT budgets will grow, and for the first time in several years, companies are able to shift from a "do more with less" to a "do more with more" IT operation. Companies are adopting new technologies to deliver new services and in some cases, to cut ongoing costs with more efficient systems.

When asked about their primary IT focus areas in the next 12 months, cloud computing, security and IT consolidation topped the charts. Of the 573 business leaders in 18 countries, 60 percent report cloud computing, 58 percent report security, and 31 percent report IT consolidation as the three highest priorities.

While 60 percent of companies worldwide said cloud computing is a top IT priority for the next year, the sentiment is even higher in the C-suite with three in four (75 percent) C-level executives reporting cloud computing as top of mind.

According to the survey, 74 percent of enterprises are using some form of cloud services. This represents a 25 percent growth since Avanade's September 2009 survey. Further, the gap between cloud adopters and those who have no plans to implement cloud computing has shrunk dramatically— 54 percent since 2009. Of the organizations that have yet to implement cloud, three-quarters say it's on the horizon.

. . . In terms of their overall IT budget, 74 percent report they have allocated up to 30 percent to cloud computing annually. For 10 percent of companies, this means spending $2 million or more on cloud computing each year. Companies

are investing in their employees too. In fact, most companies report their IT spend on cloud services is between $100 and $499 per user (38 percent).

This year (2011), additional investments in cloud services were matched by significant spending on security and training for new cloud deployments.

" . . . In terms of their overall IT budget, 74 percent report they have allocated up to 30 percent to cloud computing annually. For 10 percent of companies, this means spending $2 million or more on cloud computing each year."

Tyson Hartman is Avanade's chief technology officer. He's responsible for Avanade's technology vision, solutions, and R&D investments. As CTO, he leads the incubation and engineering teams that deliver differentiated solutions across the complete enterprise IT life cycle. I spoke with Tyson about the survey and its implications. Here's a summary of his observations:

There's been a significant turn of the tide. We're definitely past the "what and if" phase and getting into the "where and when" phase. That's especially true of SaaS, where people can perceive the value of moving e-mail, collaboration, and CRM services into the cloud. With SaaS, you get a predictable cost advantage. You know exactly how much per seat your tools are costing you. That's an attractive combination—speed to market and predictable costs.

I think the tipping point for IaaS will be a little different. The buyers are different—business people gravitate to SaaS and tech people gravitate to IaaS. With SaaS, you're buying a service that is very predictable, and you take on very little operational liability. With IaaS, you're retaining a certain amount of operational control, which means you've got more visibility, but also more liability.

PaaS offers the most potential, "because basically it's a blank sheet of paper," says Tyson. But that potential is also what's holding people back from getting more involved with PaaS. Here's more of what Tyson told me:

Compared to SaaS and IaaS, PaaS is less well defined, and I think it will take people longer to appreciate the opportunities it offers. It could be a very interesting solution for Web-intensive functions that are high cost and less predictable, such as e-commerce, where most of the installed base is using custom software.

But it will take a while for PaaS to mature and get to the point where it's providing the kind of features that an e-commerce customer would need, and it will take time for the market to understand what PaaS can offer.

If you had a pie chart showing the relative proportions of SaaS, PaaS, and IaaS customers worldwide, all I can say is that those proportions will be changing very quickly. This is a fast-moving market.

The research also shows that a strong preference is emerging for private cloud deployments, especially in areas of competitive differentiation. Here's what the report says:

Previously, companies relied on third-party public cloud providers for the majority of their cloud infrastructure. Yet today, nearly half of all companies (43 percent) report they utilize private clouds. Further, another 34 percent say they will begin to do so in the next 12 months.

Overall, 63 percent say they are ready for private cloud and the majority says it plays a role in their cloud strategy. In the C-suite, perceptions are higher with more than 70 percent saying their company is ready for private clouds. In preparation for this, companies are investing in everything from security (48 percent) to their networks (47 percent) and staff (35 percent).

While opinions vary, most see private clouds as more secure and easier to control.

I think that many of us had a gut feeling about this, and it's great to see the survey numbers supporting our instinctive sense that many companies will see private clouds as a better strategic fit than public clouds.

> **"The mandate to use cloud computing to deliver new products and services to customers is coming from the C-suite. More than one in five C-level executives believe cloud computing will increase revenues."**

The report also supports a theme that has been running through this book, namely, the idea that the cloud has great potential to help companies improve their top-line performance. Again, quoting from the report:

Companies are moving beyond internal employee-facing cloud services to use them with external customers.

Further, aggressive adopters report top-line growth as a driver for cloud deployments. The mandate to use cloud computing to deliver new products and services to customers is coming from the C-suite. More than one in five C-level executives believe cloud computing will increase revenues.

Experience suggests that as executives learn more about the cloud, they will want to review cloud options when any new technology for generating revenue is under consideration.

Translating "Speeds and Feeds" into Cash Flow

I decided to conclude this chapter by recounting a recent conversation I had with Mike Blake. Mike is the CIO at Hyatt Hotels Corp. Like most CIOs, he's comfortable talking about the technology side of his job. But he's one of a handful of CIOs who is equally comfortable talking about the financial component of his role as a C-level corporate officer.

Unlike many of his peers, Mike has a deep finance background that affords him a unique perspective on the relationship between IT and the enterprise. Before being named Hyatt's CIO, he was the company's VP of Finance Global Marketing, Brand Standards, and IT. Prior to joining Hyatt, he was SVP of Finance at First Data Corp. Before that, he was VP of Finance at Kaiser Permanente. He's a CPA and a CMA. He holds an MBA from the University of Chicago. When he describes himself as a "hardcore finance guy," he isn't exaggerating!

I asked him to describe his method for assembling a portfolio of IT services and applications. Here's a summary of what he said:

I look at investments through the lens of an ROI calculation in which the numerator is value and the denominator is cost. As CIO, my job is increasing value while reducing cost. I look at everything through that lens, which allows me to focus on the end result. I think of it as translating "speeds and feeds" into cash flow.

For example, we recently changed our e-mail system. One of the reasons we switched was that many of our employees had difficulty using the old e-mail system. As a result, there were lots of calls to the help desk. Those calls represent costs. They represent downtime and lost productivity. We factored the economics of all that into our decision to go with a new e-mail provider.

In addition to being easier to use, the new cloud-based system enables Hyatt to provide e-mail, instant messaging, and social collaboration apps for 17,000 employees and 40,000 desk-less workers such as bellhops and housekeepers. By improving connectivity across the enterprise, Hyatt improves efficiency and productivity. Guests are happier, too, because their needs are met more quickly.

Mike is continuing Hyatt's migration into the cloud, a process the company began 16 years ago. Migrating into the cloud is not a simple process—in fact, it's a lot like finance. There are plenty of variables that require continuing attention. For example, Hyatt's property management system is hosted by AT&T. The company's financial systems are hosted by Oracle. Reservations and group sales are outsourced to CSC. NaviSite, a managed cloud services provider owned by Time Warner Cable, is also part of the mix. That's a lot of complexity!

But there's an upside. Hyatt's global IT organization is genuinely lean—just forty-three people. And it's nimble. System changes can be implemented in hours, instead of days or weeks. Security is handled by the cloud providers, which removes a heavy burden from IT's shoulders. "AT&T can afford to spend a lot more on security than we can," says Mike. "And that's fine with me. I get to leverage their investments in new technology. I don't have to worry about change management issues. And as the model matures, the price comes down."

From Mike's perspective, IT is all about reducing operational costs across the business. "That's what IT does—drives down cost. The cloud can help you do that, so why not take advantage of it?"

Chapter 10

Entering the Cloud

Now, hopefully, you have an idea of what the cloud universe looks like and what it comprises. The next step is determining which IT services should stay right where they are, and which IT services should be moved into the cloud.

The best and easiest way to start is by reviewing your inventory of applications—your software portfolio.

"Look first at applications that don't require a high degree of state," says John Hill. "Look for workloads that are highly transient. Applications that utilize IT resources at a fairly consistent level should not be considered prime cloud candidates because it would be cheaper to run them in a hosted environment. Look for applications with spiky usage patterns and seasonal peaks."

John suggests this basic approach:

- Establish an application portfolio strategy.

- Embrace SaaS.

- Accelerate virtualization of applications.

- Adopt application life-cycle management (including framework selection) processes.

- Ensure SOA/Web services infrastructure is in place.

- Implement a robust service request portal to provide a consistent way for users to request cloud and traditional services.

- Implement a converged infrastructure for network/server/storage.

- Establish a cross-discipline architecture and engineering team to guide cloud efforts.

- Pilot and experiment; figure out what works and scale it.

- Focus on creating business value!

David Linthicum outlines this high-level, four-step process in his book:

1. List candidate platforms (for migration to the cloud).

2. Analyze and test candidate platforms.

3. Select target platforms.

4. Deploy to target platforms.

Steve Phillpott, the CIO at Amylin Pharmaceuticals, used a three-step process that looks like this:

1. Review portfolio of IT services *and* their costs.

2. Rationalize and prioritize services against appropriate cloud use cases.

3. Move IT services into the cloud—when appropriate.

Let's drill down into the first two steps. Step 1, for example, includes a detailed breakout of IT services. Here's a snippet that will give you an idea of the detail in Steve's analysis:

IM Services	Total Cost of Individual Service	Individual % of Total Budget
Technology Infrastructure Engineering and Operations		
Communications		
Directory Services and E-mail (including LO)		
Phones/Phone Sys/Voicemail		
Conf Room Equip & Support		
Web-Voice-Video Conf		
Telecommunications Services		
Wired—WAN/LAN and Internet Transport		
Wireless Telecomm Services		
Remote Access Enablement		
InfoSec/Risk Mgmt/DR/SOX		
End User Computing		
Desktop Computing HW SW Engineering		
Personal Printers/Shared Printers/ Copiers		
Service Desk and User Support		
Service Desk Operations		
Executive Support		
Event Support (Site Mtgs, ADA)		

(continued)

(Continued)

IM Services	Total Cost of Individual Service	Individual % of Total Budget
Technology Infrastructure Engineering and Operations		
Site Support		
Enterprise Collaboration Services		
LiveLink EDMS		
Collab Services SPoint/MOSS and Content Mgmt		

Here is a breakout of criteria used to complete Step 2:

Cost/Benefit ROI (TCO-Based)
Performance and Architecture Fit
Control/Governance Data Mgmt, Customization, etc.
Security/Risk Mgmt Privacy, Compliance, etc.

For Steve, it was critical to develop (and follow) a practical decision matrix process. As you recall from the story he tells earlier in the book (see Chapter 9), he and his team had spent months developing a "cost-by-services" IT budget model that would enable them to make apples-to-apples comparisons between the costs of traditional on-premises solutions and cloud-based services.

They looked for—and found—TCO reductions of 30 to 70 percent. They also factored in the advantages of variable costs (as opposed to fixed costs), shorter implementation times, automatic upgrades (at no incremental cost), and improved functionality. They also added the value "recovered" by shifting IT resources from low-value tactical activities (such as maintenance) to higher-value strategic activities (such as planning and partnering with the business).

I boiled part of Steve's process down to a checklist:

	On-Premises Solution	Off-Premises Solution (cloud or other form of outsourcing)
TFO	*Higher*	*Lower*
Costs based on demand	*No, costs are fixed*	*Yes, costs are variable*
Automatic upgrades	*No (and they're expensive)*	*Yes (and they're free)*
Time to implementation	*Longer, slower*	*Shorter, faster*
IT focus	*Tactical*	*Strategic*

The point of all these charts isn't to create headaches or accounting nightmares—the point is to illustrate the granularity of data required to reach the best possible decisions about which services to move into the cloud. In these kinds of situations, the last thing you want to do is rely on guesswork or hunches. You really have to do your homework. As Pat Toole mentioned earlier, this isn't rocket science—but it is computer science!

Governance Is Fundamental to Success

We all have a tendency to look at governance as a set of limits or restrictions, a list of directives all beginning with "Thou shalt not . . . " I prefer to look at governance as a framework, or as a map. It shows you where borders are. It says, "Here is safe ground, here is unsafe ground."

My conversation with John Hill reminded me that governance can be leveraged to increase acceptance and utilization of new technology. When you have clear governance policies, people are less afraid to embrace new ideas and new ways of doing things.

For cloud initiatives, governance is absolutely critical. Since a key attribute of the cloud is self-service, people need to know the rules and have a fundamental understanding of the boundaries. In other words, you need an ultra-clear set of written policies for using cloud services.

Here is where your role as an executive leader comes into play again. You will have to designate a team to write a set of cloud policies. You will have to spell out the policies clearly and unambiguously. After the team has written its first draft, you will have to review it carefully to ensure that your policies aren't so draconian that they will deter people from using cloud services.

Remember, the point of having written policies isn't to prevent people from using cloud services—the reason you create a set of policies is to give people a sense of safety and security. The policies are there to say, in effect, "As long as you do this and avoid doing that, nothing bad will happen."

Just posting the policies somewhere on your corporate intranet won't be sufficient. You will have to hold training sessions—they can be live sessions, webinars, video conference calls, and so on. The point is training users to see the policies as a helpful guide, and not as a burden.

And of course, the policies have to be written into the automation process. That's what I meant earlier when we were talking about "policy-driven" provisioning of cloud services. Ideally, provisioning of cloud services should be through an automated self-service portal. It should be easy, immediate, and measurable. It should also conform to your written policies.

When you assemble your policy development team, make sure to include representatives from other areas of the enterprise, such as legal, HR, sales, finance—any area where you anticipate usage of cloud services. The perspectives and opinions of people outside of IT can be extremely useful when writing an enterprise-wide policy. Including a diverse range of perspectives in the policy development process is more than just good management—it will help you avoid problems down the road.

Due Diligence

We asked several of our sources to list the due diligence questions every CIO should ask before moving an IT service into the cloud. We got great responses from everyone we asked, and we picked the best two to share with you.

We'll begin with Trae Chancellor, VP of Global Enterprise Strategy at Salesforce.com. In addition to *providing* cloud services, Salesforce.com also *uses* cloud services. Trae, who initially joined Salesforce.com as its CIO, recounted the story of the company's transformation from traditional IT to a cloud-based services model. The transformation project began in 2006 and took about two years to complete. Here is a summary of what he told me:

> *When we began our transformation, platform-as-a-service didn't exist. We took our IT department and moved it into R&D. We decided that everything we required from a platform from an IT perspective would be built natively in the platform that we were continually developing, which eventually became Force.com. The idea of sandboxes (environments for development, testing, and training without compromising data and applications in the production environment) and open architecture all came out of that transformation.*

> *For us, a key piece of the process was being able to promote changes from the sandbox to production. Initially, we had to do that manually. Now we can do it with a click. I've seen companies set up test environments and then begin integration with key systems within a couple of weeks and drive innovation. It really comes down to how fast your people can make the transformation and ensure balance between pace and governance.*

> *The big lesson that I learned from all of this is that transformation into the cloud is a people issue—a change management issue—and not a technology issue. The technology is there, it's available. The issue is speed and pace. How fast can your people adapt to change and innovation? That's the issue. Sometimes I wish that I had taken more psychology classes in college. Moving into the cloud isn't about technology—it's about leadership. You have to be a leader to help people make the transformation.*

> "The big lesson that I learned from all of this is that transformation into the cloud is a people issue—a change management issue—and not a technology issue."

This is exactly the kind of insight that CIOs need to hear and internalize: Leadership makes or breaks a transformation strategy.

Here is Trae's list of due diligence steps:

1. Confer with your peers; let them tell you what works and what doesn't.

2. Make sure that your cloud provider is ready for a long-term partnership. Make sure that you're dealing with a reliable, established provider with a track record of supporting their customers and enabling their success.

3. Always remember the basic value proposition of the cloud: faster innovation and reduced complexity. Make sure the provider can deliver on the foundational promise of cloud technology (i.e., speed, simplicity, agility).

4. Make sure your provider innovates *faster* than you can—you don't want to develop a great new product and then find out that your cloud provider can't deliver the service required to get that product or service to market.

5. Avoid the possibility of vendor lock-in by choosing providers whose cloud services are built on open standards

and open architectures. In the long run, vendor lock-in will add cost, reduce your agility, and slow your pace of innovation.

This advice is priceless, and I'm grateful to Trae for sharing the lessons he learned as a genuine cloud pioneer.

I'm also delighted that Tony Leng agreed to share his list of essential due diligence questions with us. Tony is a Managing Director at Diversified Search and heads up the Technology, CIO and Private Equity practices within the firm. Prior to his executive search experience, Tony served on the board of three public companies and was the CEO of a $600 million public diversified IT company that controlled businesses in software, communications, services, distribution, integration, defense technology, and outsourcing. Before that, Tony ran a large division of a major telco focused on corporate users and had responsibility for all data services and networking products.

Tony's list is gleaned from his frequent exposure to CIOs and begins with three broad areas of consideration, followed by two sets of due diligence questions, one focused on internal issues and the other focused on external issues.

Three Broad Concerns

1. **Security.** For certain industries, security is a big issue. For example insurance is a regulated industry and they also handle personal information. Currently I know of CIOs who are not convinced that there is an acceptably secure solution outside a private cloud.

2. **Service levels.** Many online companies have to be available 24/7 365 days a year. Again, outside a private cloud, I have yet to hear of a service provider that can provide that level of service. Since the cost is also tied to service levels, pushing for 99.999 uptime can become very expensive.

3. **Cost of the service.** The true value of the cloud to one CIO I know is that his company has high and low usage levels on a daily basis with a significant difference in the computing power required at peak times. They also have seasonal highs and lows with the same profile. Therefore, a metered cloud is theoretically very attractive to him, but it is very hard to find a service provider that can mirror his environment where the cost is less than his current internal cost. (Note: these arguments do not apply as much to a pre-production environment.)

Next come the due diligence questions a CIO should ask after deciding that an external cloud provider is in fact viable for the organization.

Looking Internally:

1. What are your strengths and what is strategic? For example, for most companies a data center is not unique or strategic, which will make the infrastructure a candidate for cloud.

2. What is the appetite (culturally) for your organization to move systems, data, processes, applications into the cloud?

3. What data is governed by compliance/regulatory requirements? Not everything in an IT organization is subject to regulation.

4. What does your cost structure look like?

5. Can IT become a contributor to the top line if resources are deployed more effectively?

Looking Externally:

1. How mature is the provider in providing services?

2. What is your exit strategy in case the relationship with the provider goes south? Think about this *before* committing.

3. SLAs are a given . . . but becoming less important. An SLA with someone you don't trust is just a source of strife. You need to decide if and how you can build trust with your provider.

4. When evaluating a provider, talk to other clients using the same service at your scale. Industry is generally not important for this conversation.

5. What are the scale boundaries for the services you are using? How big can they really go? Not just what they say . . . you have to validate it.

6. How would you use a multivendor strategy for each service moving into the cloud? How well do the providers work together? How much does your architecture have to change to accommodate this methodology?

7. Review the provider Disaster Recovery plan. Ask to see the latest test.

8. How easy is it to extend the solution, can you do it yourself, or do you have to pay your provider to make extensions?

9. Does the provider have an app exchange that will let you add extensions or other solutions easily?

10. Ask to see the release schedule of future releases and ask how often the releases are done.

11. How often does the provider take the cloud solution down for maintenance?

12. Who are their implementation partners (if they have any)?

13. Does the platform scale? Is it really designed to be a multitenancy app, or is it just a hosted solution called a cloud service?

14. Understand the difference between infrastructure-as-a-service (IaaS), platform-as-a-service (PaaS), and software-as-a-service (SaaS). They all have a place and are all different. What is the provider offering?

> **You have to embrace failure. Embrace chaos while you're at it too. There's the concept of "chaos monkey." It really puts the team in a mode of expecting failure and therefore it changes your paradigm and frees you of historical encumbrances.**

I also asked Tony to weigh in on two general questions about the cloud and IT leadership. Here are his unedited responses, in a Q&A format:

Question: Tony, what have your experiences with major trends similar to the cloud taught you, and what advice do you have for companies considering cloud-based services?

Answer:

- If you don't have a cloud strategy, you're already behind the curve. But as an organization crafts its cloud strategy, it must take into account the impact of executing that strategy, both internally and externally.

- The CIO should first evaluate the strategic advantage of a move to cloud-based services. Does it make sense to do it now?

- Moving to the cloud is not simply moving a service from an internal provider to an external provider. Most of the initial challenges involve overcoming organizational hurdles.

- Cultural change should thus be addressed as one of the first agenda items and is fundamentally a leadership issue.

- Architectural changes are also important. You can't just assume that operating in the cloud works the same as it did internally. In most cases, it doesn't.

- Embrace failure. Embrace chaos while you're at it too. There's the concept of "chaos monkey." It really puts the team in a mode of expecting failure and therefore it changes your paradigm and frees you of historical encumbrances. This doesn't mean you have to fail, but until the market matures there will be some bumps along the road.

- A good comparison is the cross over from physical to virtual environments that have taken place over the past few years. If you look at the early adopters who took on virtualization when the software was relatively immature, it is clear they had a number of issues to overcome. But when the supporting software and processes matured, it made adoption of virtualization a lot easier and more pain free. Looking at the adoption of cloud services, you see a similar trend. The software and process are improving and should reach maturity soon. Companies must look at their own profiles, their ability to accept risk, and the level of security they require, and then make a decision as to whether "the cloud" is ready for them. As one CIO told me, "Looking at the graph for cloud adoption we decided it was too early for our company."

- You need to be prepared for updates three times a year. You often don't have a choice; you just get the updates.

- Experience skills sets in these new platforms are new, expensive, and harder to find.

- It will eliminate capital cost, but that capital cost will be replaced by monthly/yearly operating costs forever. This could be good or bad depending if you are capital budget constrained or operating budget constrained.

Q: From your perspective, what are the main leadership challenges facing CIOs in a rapidly changing business environment?

Answer:

1. The challenges vary by industry, company size, and age. For a mature company, with mainframes and large staffs, the challenge is very different than for a newer, agile, innovative company. Here are some typical challenges to overcome.

2. There is FUD (Fear, Uncertainty, and Doubt). There are many different models that range from avoiding cloud to jumping in head-first. I think the first challenge is fear of the unknown. You can't avoid it because, if you do, the business will work around CIOs and IT organizations to get what they need. This is a leadership challenge.

3. The CIO also needs to be able to truly think strategically and talk business . . . not technology. Many CIOs say they can do this . . . but it is still a major challenge. The CIO needs to be driving the process or it will happen around him/her; yet another leadership challenge.

4. The CIO must get the IT team to embrace cloud. They may look at it (like outsourcing years back) as a job-elimination plan for the infrastructure group. It's not. Cloud solutions provide a significant opportunity for the IT organization to become more strategic and business focused; yet another leadership challenge. And it's a great way to move dollars toward revenue-generation activities that support the top line.

5. One CIO I know says that his challenges are on two main fronts, "more with less" and "time to market." Hidden in these are the challenges of mobile computing, the cloud, virtualization, big data, and licensing. (You need to be very aware of the "gotchas" in licensing as you move to offshoring, working from home, and remote computing.)

From this, it is clear that cloud is one part of a complex array of strategic challenges and choices facing CIOs, but it is a vital one, and the right choice can ensure that the CIO is a tremendous contributor to building business value.

It's great that Tony could take the time to join the conversation and provide such helpful responses.

Taking "No" Off the Table

When Clifton (Clif) Triplett confronts a complex IT challenge, he often reflects on his 10-year career as a U.S. Army officer. "Saying 'no' was not an option," says Clif. "We were expected to build systems that could survive being blown up or infiltrated."

> "You have to assume the potential for compromise or failure and design your systems so they'll still work, even if something goes wrong. That's life; you just have to take life as it is dealt and take the challenges head on."

Today Clif is VP and CIO at Baker Hughes, a global provider of advanced technology and consulting services to the oil and gas industry. A graduate of the U.S. Military Academy at West Point, Clif still finds his Army experience beneficial, especially when the challenges seem daunting or insurmountable. Here are some of the unique insights that Clif shared with me, in his own words:

In the military, you operate under the assumption that some resources might be lost or compromised. You have to assume that your assets will come and go, and that you won't always have full control over the operational environment.

That's why you have to make the best use of all of the available resources. Let's say you're in the field artillery. You have four guns and the enemy is approaching. Are you only going to use one gun? How many do you want to hold in reserve? Three are probably too many.

When I think of cloud computing, I see it from a similar perspective. You have to assume the potential for compromise or failure and design your systems so they'll still work, even if something goes wrong. That's life; you just have to take life as it is dealt and take the challenges head on.

Cloud computing is at our doorstep. Even though a cloud service could cause problems or because the provider won't guarantee 100 percent availability, I will figure out how to make the best use of the asset as it exists and see what I can do to improve on it.

Security is another issue that often slows the adoption of available cloud resources. I asked Clif how he would reply if someone on his team expressed doubts about security. Here's what he said:

Our cloud security strategy is fairly robust, so I don't think my security leader would say we cannot use cloud services because we do not know how to leverage it safely. But it would not surprise me to hear him say he's discovered a new threat vector that has arisen and concerns him. In that case, I'd probably ask, "Which dimension of our defenses bothers you? Is the problem preventing, detecting, containing, or eradicating the threat?"

Very quickly and very methodically, we would get into a very specific conversation about the problem and the solution. And of course, it's important to have a common taxonomy so we can all understand each other.

I am deeply impressed by the combination of common sense, leadership skill, and executive ability that Clif brings to the table. He embodies the "can-do" purposeful spirit that we often strive to achieve in ourselves. Here's some great advice he offered during our conversation:

Essentially, we have to stop asking, "Can it be done?" and start asking, "How can it be done?" Our team and our suppliers have accomplished some remarkable things because I've asked them to aim higher. If you play the victim, then maybe all you can get is 98.5 percent availability guaranteed. But if you partner with people and provide leadership, you can get 100 percent.

Leadership is the key, says Clif. The problem, he says, is that many people still cling to the past. They find it difficult to accept that the world around them is continuously changing and transforming. As a result, they tend to look backward for answers, instead of forward. Here is Clif's take on the dichotomy:

In IT, we used to sit around waiting for orders. We can't do that any more. We need to be out there pushing what's possible. Yes, the business needs to tell us what it needs to do and where it wants to go. But we really have to make sure that the conversation is about capabilities and outcomes, and not about technical gobbledygook.

I'm constantly pushing my team to go faster than the speed of business. In the past, IT was always a barrier. Now IT is an enabler. We enable the business to innovate. We want the business to have the capabilities it needs to innovate—sometimes before the business even knows that it needs those capabilities!

To me, being the CIO is about continuous improvement. We never want to move backward. That means pushing people to move forward, which is a skill in itself. In fact, it's the secret sauce—moving people forward.

But you have to know how hard to push. And that means you have to talk to people, get to know them, and discover their passion. Passion is the most important thing. Passion is contagious, and it's the key to success.

"In the past, IT was always a barrier. Now IT is an enabler. We enable the business to innovate."

Clif's ability to motivate people—and to form meaningful partnerships with them—has led to some incredible successes with suppliers such as IBM and Microsoft. "I try to create win-win situations, where we all focus on the mission," he says. "We play as a team and we all share our ideas. We know we have to achieve results because the team has to establish a track record of delivering value consistently."

"To me, being the CIO is about continuous improvement. We never want to move backward. That means pushing people to move forward, which is a skill in itself. In fact, it's the secret sauce—moving people forward."

Clif sometimes refers to the "3Cs" of successful leadership as *communications, candy,* and *cadence:*

1. **Communications.** Be engaged, reflect priorities, demonstrate understanding, discuss priorities, offer choices, review trade-offs, and communicate status updates, issues, and wins.

2. **Candy.** Do not underestimate the value perceived from unexpected, easy, low-cost activities.

3. **Cadence.** Establish a reputation for predictable and reliable delivery of value.

He also has a great acronym from his Army career: BLUF, which stands for Bottom Line Up Front. Basically, it means deliver your message simply and clearly. Don't beat around the bush. Don't make people guess what's important, and don't make them wait for the punch line. Lay out the intent and then build on it. "And always remember," says Clif, "once you've sold it—move on."

When you talk about the cloud with the CEO or the board, don't get lost in the technical details—talk about the result and the value you plan to deliver. Don't talk about the technology itself—talk instead about how the technology will help the organization overcome specific business challenges or achieve stated objectives.

"Bring the conversation home and talk to people about the specific problem you're solving," says Clif. "Stay focused on the outcome."

AFTERWORD: SPEND MORE TIME LEADING THE IT ORGANIZATION AND LESS TIME WORRYING ABOUT AGING CAPITAL EQUIPMENT

I thought it would be a nice idea to end the book with excerpts from three interesting interviews that I conducted in the summer of 2011. All three of the interviews focus on the value of seasoned leadership in the IT organization.

Let's begin with Bert Odinet. Bert is the Global CIO at Freeport-McMoRan Copper & Gold. Freeport, a Fortune 500 company, has operations in the North America, South America, Europe, Asia, and Africa. Freeport is the world's largest publicly traded producer of copper and molybdenum. And it's the single largest taxpayer in Indonesia, where it owns the world's largest copper and gold mine in terms of recoverable reserves.

I cite these statistics to show the scope, scale, and complexity of Freeport's operations. In 2007, Freeport acquired copper producer Phelps Dodge. Major acquisitions almost always involve major integration efforts, and Bert's role as CIO made him a key player in the process.

In this case, the timing of the acquisition, and the subsequent need for an enterprise-wide integration process, led the company to make what I believe were some truly inspired choices. Here's the story in Bert's own words:

179

Both companies were spread wide geographically. The combined business had operations on every major continent. We knew that we had to globalize our processes. As we thought about how to do that, we started looking at all of our redundant core back office systems.

And when we looked down the silos of the business processes—whether it was HR, commercial, or supply chain—they didn't necessarily fit very well. We didn't have one existing solution that would scale for everyone.

A new ERP system seemed like the wisest choice. But there were other factors, such as legacy infrastructure and applications.

Our hardware platform was late in its life cycle, especially on the server side. The chip set was getting old. We knew we had to port the core operating system and the applications. It was the equivalent of replacing the engine and the transmission in an old car. At some point, it makes more sense to buy a new car.

We also wanted to get out of the data center business, which meant doing a data center migration. When we looked at everything we needed to do—implement an ERP, new platform, data center migration—it all seemed like too much to accomplish using traditional approaches.

And now the story gets *really* interesting. Instead of doing it the old-fashioned way, Bert and his team decided to host the new systems in a private cloud. In addition to saving money and avoiding the headaches of managing their own data center, their cloud strategy would greatly accelerate the pace of the projects. Bert's previous experience with mainframe-to-client/server conversions back in the 1990s gave him the confidence and the knowledge he needed to move forward with the cloud option.

The guiding principles are the same. If you can quickly provision an environment, then you have a lot more options. You can have multiple versions running at once. Each developer can potentially have his or her own versions, and each testing group can have their own version. So the planning and scheduling of a giant integrated project becomes much simpler.

In a typical ERP project, you might be limited by sheer physical resources to seven or eight environments; if one group is testing something and they want to take a checkpoint and go back to the data as it existed two days before, then everyone else had to take that checkpoint, too. That requires an immense amount of forward planning.

Creating multiple environments in the cloud takes coordination, but it also gives you a lot of freedom, which then allows you to accomplish things you couldn't ordinarily do.

A perfect example was in our conversion testing. We had three environments running in parallel, with the same data. Environment A was the first run; environment B followed it by a few hours and environment C followed that one by a few hours. The team would run the conversion program for a few hours in environment A and when we found we had problems, we could fix it in environment B before it ran into those problems. In the old model, you used to have to take a checkpoint, fix your problems, restore the data, you lose a day or so getting back to that point. You have to re-run those jobs all over again—only to find out that you had another problem!

The goal, says Bert, is eliminating the interdependencies.

*As these projects scale up, they become more and more compli-
cated. The larger the system is, the more modules and the more
people involved—it gets exponentially more complicated and
more expensive.*

*In an ERP implementation, you might have 300 people on
the project team. If you need to keep all of them in sync, you
will need to do a lot of upfront planning. But if everyone is
free to do their own thing, you can do a lot less planning, and
the project will go a lot faster.*

*You will have the ability to do more testing and really make
sure the data is clean. Remember, this isn't just about the project schedule—it's also about what happens after you cut over
to the new system. There's a huge difference between being
99.99% ready and being 98% ready. With 99.99%, you have
a smooth stable system. With 98%, you have a mess that rapidly becomes very difficult to manage.*

From Bert's perspective, the cloud was "a consequence"—
a means to an end, not an end in itself.

*The ERP system doesn't even know that it's running in the
cloud. For us, the cloud enabled an important business process transformation that, in turn, enabled the company to
move forward more quickly. The cloud doesn't drive our business decisions—but it's helping us achieve our business goals,
faster and more economically.*

Leveraging the Cloud to Drive Integration

The upside of free markets is that they typically bring out the
best in everyone. The downside is that free markets are
crowded with vendors who compete for your business. That's
good and bad for CIOs. The good part is that you have more

choice and more leverage over pricing. The bad part is that each vendor sells products that are different from the products sold by its competitors. And that means that you, the CIO, has to make sure that all of those different product work together seamlessly.

Nicholas Colisto is VP and CIO at Hovnanian Enterprises, Inc., one of the nation's largest residential homebuilders. Before joining Hovnanian, he held key information technology leadership positions at large organizations, including Pepsi-Cola, Priceline.com, Hyperion Solutions, Boehringer-Ingelheim, and Bayer Corporation (formerly Sterling Winthrop). He's seen the IT landscape from a variety of perspectives, which makes him a valuable source of insight.

Like many CIOs, Nick faced the task of integrating numerous disparate systems into one common company system. Here's the story in his own words:

When I joined the company in 2005, it had already made multiple acquisitions over the years. The company was very entrepreneurial and highly decentralized. The CEO wanted a common operating platform so we could harmonize business processes across the company. When we rolled out national marketing programs, we wanted to make sure they were consistent across our markets. When the business units prepared their financial reports, we wanted them to be uniform across the company. We also wanted our IT systems to be standard and highly available. The companies we acquired had their own IT systems, each with its own set of applications and infrastructure.

Nick established a governance model, including a series of process leadership committees, to establish a standard set of business processes designed to increase sales, improve profit, and enhance customer satisfaction across the company. IT joined in the process design efforts, and led the initiative to select software best suited to satisfy the new business requirements. After several years of hard work by many employees across the company, an integrated suite of systems and processes (including ERP, CRM, SCM, and BI) was delivered to the business. The suite is called KHISS (the acronym for K. Hovnanian's Integrated Software System) and it's now used by more than 1,600 employees across the company. The system has helped Nick and his team earn accolades within the company as well as externally. Over the last few years, Hovnanian Enterprises, Inc., has been recognized with seven IT industry awards, including CIO 100 by *CIO* Magazine, ComputerWorld's Premier 100, InfoWorld 100, and InformationWeek 100, among others.

To achieve the agility and speed required to complete the project successfully, Nick leveraged the cloud—50 percent of the solution is hosted remotely using a SaaS model.

Going to the cloud really helped us accelerate the delivery of the enterprise solution. It gave us much more agility by helping us to rapidly and inexpensively provision software and infrastructure resources. We didn't have to concern ourselves with setting up all the different environments—development, test, production, fail-over, etc. We were able to get up to speed very quickly with a comprehensive solution, which is hosted on private and public clouds.

Disaster recovery was built into the solution as well. Integration is the circulatory system of KHISS and we were very successful in achieving interoperability with our hybrid

*deployment model of public and private clouds. We were orig-
inally concerned about security, but we discovered that security actually improved through centralization of data and
increased security-focused resources. Additionally, the solution required fewer IT skills internally. We also have a lot
more reliability with the platform and it's much more scalable
than our previous disparate systems that were all hosted internally. Maintenance of the cloud computing applications is a
lot easier because they don't need to be installed on desktops—
it's all Internet-based.*

This is a great example of how a savvy CIO can leverage
the cloud to drive integration across the enterprise. Nick and
his team use the cloud to streamline business processes and
drive down costs. It's a classic case of IT helping the business
solve problems and overcome challenges. To me, that's smart
leadership.

It's All about Leadership

I'm delighted that my conversations with Bert and Nick
brought us back to the topic of leadership, which is still the
core responsibility of the CIO.

A few weeks before wrapping up the manuscript, I had a
great conversation with my good friend Mark Polansky. Mark,
as many of you know, is Senior Client Partner and Managing
Director of the IT Officers Practice at Korn/Ferry International. From his post at Korn/Ferry, Mark has a genuinely
unique view of the evolving role of the CIO in the modern
enterprise. He also knows what CEOs and executive boards
look for when they are hiring a new CIO. Here are some nuggets of advice that Mark shared with me:

No matter how fast the technology landscape changes and shifts, nothing beats good old fashioned leadership. You can improve your leadership skills with a combination of formal and informal training. Make sure you're getting 360-degree feedback. And don't be afraid to look in the mirror.

Create the time for mentoring, in both directions. Find a mentor for yourself, even if you're a CIO reporting to the CEO. Find a mentor on the board, or find a mentor from another company—maybe the CIO at a bigger company. And make sure that the people who report to you have mentors . . .

One of the biggest challenges facing CIOs is developing the leadership skills of those behind them. Some of the world's best CIOs measure their success by the number of people who have worked for them and then went on to become CIOs themselves.

I really like how Mark frames the CIO's role in terms of executive leadership instead of technology management. As Mark says, CIOs have rightfully earned their seat at the table. The enterprise needs their leadership—especially in today's uncertain times.

The Beginning of the Cloud Era

The cloud raises many significant technology questions. But for the modern transformational CIO, here is one question that trumps them all: Would you prefer spending your time leading the IT organization and helping the company grow, or tending an unruly tangle of legacy systems?

The cloud offers you an escape from the endless cycle of upgrading and replacing capital equipment. The cloud lets you focus on providing services instead of providing systems.

Yes, it's a whole new way of looking at IT. The old IT paradigm was about processes; the new IT paradigm is about results. The cloud simply offers the fastest path to the new paradigm.

Does that mean the cloud is the end of IT? Not by a long shot. The cloud represents another stage in the evolution of technology. I look at the cloud as a bridge that gets us from where we are to where we want to be.

I am also convinced that the cloud's moment has arrived, and that the cloud will be with us for a while. Here's why I believe the cloud will continue growing for at least the next decade.

Despite all the dire headlines and genuine distress about various regional economies, the global economy is growing. People all over the world are becoming wealthier. The most obvious indicator of this new wealth is the growth of mobile phone usage. We're experiencing the greatest transformation of human culture since the invention of the printing press, but because we're right in the middle of it, we can't perceive the enormity of the changes.

The explosive growth of mobile is driving the explosive growth of social media, which in turn is driving the explosive growth of Big Data. Make no mistake: We are now generating new data at astonishing speed and unimaginable magnitude. As a global culture, we have created a deluge of data. There's no place for all of this new data to go except into the cloud.

Big Data is driving the cloud *and will continue to drive the cloud*, because Big Data is simply *too big* to exist on any single system. Big Data is destined to live in the cloud because it can't live anywhere else.

If your company depends on data—and it's hard to imagine a company that doesn't—you need a cloud strategy, today. Maybe 10 or 20 years from now, we'll invent a newer technology that will make the cloud obsolete. That day will come, no doubt. But for the now, smart money is betting on the cloud.

MEET OUR SOURCES

Rich Adduci

Rich Adduci joined Boston Scientific in 2006 as Boston Scientific's chief information officer (CIO). In his role as CIO, Rich has led the transformation of Boston Scientific's IS organization, creating a Global IS organization focused on delivering competitive advantage for Boston Scientific through information and technology.

Rich serves as a member of Boston Scientific's Operating Committee, Quality Management Board, and Capital Committee. Rich is actively engaged in shaping direction in the information technology community at large through his active participation in the SAP Life Sciences Advisory Committee, Model N Strategic Planning Team, and the Babson CIMS Advisory Board. Prior to joining Boston Scientific, Rich was a partner at Accenture.

Rich earned a bachelor of science in industrial engineering from Purdue University and an MBA from the University of Chicago with concentrations in finance and economics. Rich is an active member of his community and presently serves on the Boston area American Heart Association executive board.

Ramón Baez

Ramón Baez has been chief information officer and vice president for information technology services of Kimberly-Clark Corp. since February 15, 2007. He is responsible for leading Kimberly-Clark's enterprise-wide information systems initiatives to support its future growth and to maximize the return on its information technology investments.

Ramón began his career at Northrop Grumman Corporation. He served as chief information officer of Thermo Fisher Scientific, Inc., where he was responsible for coordinating and directing worldwide information systems. Ramón also served as chief information officer and vice president for Information Technology of Honeywell International Automation and Control Solutions group, where he led the Global IT organization of this diversified industrial, service, and solutions company. He serves as a member of the National Advisory Board at HMG Strategy LLC. Ramón holds a bachelor of science degree in business administration from University of La Verne in California.

Mike Blake

Mike Blake came to the Hyatt CIO role from his prior position as vice president of finance for global marketing, brand standards & IT for Hyatt Corporation. Mike has over 20 years of experience in finance and technology in various roles and is charged with providing strategic leadership and sound perspective that contributes to the management and evolution of Hyatt's global IT functions. He is responsible for driving innovation and supporting revenue growth.

Prior to his role with Hyatt, Mike was senior vice president of IT for First Data, vice president of IT finance at Kaiser Permanente, and director of IT finance for Sears, based in Chicago, Illinois. In each of his roles, he was the highest-ranking IT finance resource and key internal consultant and advisor to national senior leadership teams. Prior to that, Mike was director of financial planning & analysis for Commerx, a B2B startup, and director of financial planning for United Airlines.

Becky Blalock

Becky Blalock is the former senior vice president and chief information officer of Southern Company, where she directed information technology strategy and operations across 120,000 square miles and nine subsidiaries. In her role as CIO, she led more than 1,100 employees in information technology delivery at one of America's most respected companies. Becky provided broad leadership in many positions including accounting, finance, marketing, corporate communication, external affairs, the office of the CEO, and customer service.

A graduate of Leadership Atlanta and Leadership Georgia, she was named a Fellow of the International Women's Forum Leadership Foundation in 2001. Becky has received a host of honors, including 2009 CIO of the Year in the electric utility industry by *Energy Biz* magazine, 2007 CIO of the Year by Computers for Youth, and 2003 Georgia CIO of the Year,

Global Category by the Georgia CIO Leadership Association. She is listed among the Who's Who in Science and Engineering. In 2006, she was inducted as one of *Computerworld* magazine's Premier 100 IT Leaders. *Atlanta Woman* magazine named her their Power Woman of the Year and she received the Shining Star Award from the Atlanta Women's Foundation. She successfully completed the Program for Management Development at Harvard University. She holds a master's degree with honors in business administration from Mercer University and an undergraduate degree in business administration from State University of West Georgia.

Brian Bonner is the chief information officer at Texas Instruments. He is responsible for global management of all aspects of IT and is a member of the company's strategic leadership team.

Brian Bonner

Prior to becoming CIO at Texas Instruments, he served as the company's vice president, analog acquisition integrations. Before that, he was the company's vice president, worldwide mass marketing.

He is a graduate of The Fuqua School of Business at Duke University. Brian began his professional career as an engineer at Chrysler and joined Texas Instruments in 1995. In addition to his MBA, he holds a bachelor's degree in physics from Kalamazoo College and a master's degree in electrical engineering from the University of Michigan.

Robert B. (Rob) Carter

Robert B. (Rob) Carter is executive vice president of FedEx Information Services and chief information officer of FedEx Corp. He is a member of the five-person executive committee, which plans and executes the corporation's strategic business activities. He is responsible for setting technology direction, as well as the corporation's key applications and technology infrastructure. FedEx applications, advanced networks, and data centers provide around-the-clock and around-the-globe support for the product offerings of FedEx. Rob joined FedEx in 1993 and has over 30 years of systems development and implementation experience.

Rob was born in Taiwan. He earned his bachelor's degree in computer and information science from the University of Florida and his master's degree from the University of South Florida. His professional awards include: *Fast Company* magazine named #18 on "100 Most Creative People in Business" (2010); *Information Week* Chief of the Year Award (2000, 2001, 2005); *CIO* magazine's 100 Award (2000, 2001, 2002, 2003, 2004, 2006); and *InfoWorld* Chief Technology Officer of the Year (2000). He is a member of the Saks Inc. board of directors and the University of Florida Foundation board of trustees. Rob also serves as chairman of the capital campaign for the University of Tennessee Hamilton Eye Institute and as a member of the Memphis Riverfront Development Corporation and the Life-Blood Foundation.

Trae Chancellor

Trae Chancellor is the VP of global enterprise strategy of Salesforce.com. He joined Salesforce.com as CIO in 2006. Under his leadership, the IT division successfully transitioned its operations to the cloud. Building on Salesforce.com's own platform as a service, Force.com, Trae and his team deployed new automation systems that effectively supported the business as it grew from $400 million in annual revenue to $1 billion.

In his current role, Trae shares his experience of "taking it to the cloud" with large enterprises, helping them construct best-practices models for successfully adopting cloud-based computing. Additionally, Trae will transform these best practices into market-meeting requirements for Salesforce.com's emerging applications and development platform.

In 2009, Trae won *Information Week*'s top innovator award in high tech and was number five overall for his leadership in cloud computing and IT transformation. Prior to Salesforce.com, Trae was VP of IT application engineering at PeopleSoft/Oracle. While there, he drove the implementation of enterprise client/server applications for the business. Trae also led the team responsible for merging J.D. Edwards' IT environment into PeopleSoft. As a pioneer in software-as-a-service (SaaS) technology and operational models, Trae was part of the original engineering team at ExpertCity (acquired by Citrix) who built GoTo-MyPC and GoToMeeting.

Trae holds a BS degree in nuclear engineering from Texas A&M.

Nicholas R. Colisto is a senior information technology executive with experience providing innovative, business-driven IT solutions. He serves as the vice president and chief information officer at Hovnanian Enterprises, Inc., a large residential homebuilder.

Nicholas R. Colisto

Prior to joining Hovnanian, Colisto held key information technology leadership positions at large organizations, including Pepsi-Cola, Priceline.com, Hyperion Solutions, Boehringer-Ingelheim, and Bayer Corporation (formerly Sterling Winthrop).

Colisto is very active in the information technology, education, and health care communities. He has served on the Governing Body for the CIO Leadership Network and has been a speaker at the executive summits. He is a member of the Society for Information Management (SIM) and has served on its programs committee. Colisto taught a master's program in information technology at Manhattanville College in New York for several years and also served on its advisory board. He lectured at Columbia University's CIO Leadership Workshop. He currently serves on the Industrial Advisory Board at Rutgers University, on the Educational Advisory Board at Brookdale College in New Jersey, and on the Foundation Board of Trustees for Bayshore Community Hospital.

He is the recipient of many industry awards, including the 2011 *Computerworld* Premier 100 IT Leaders Award, 2010 CIO 100 by IDG's *CIO* Magazine, 2009 InfoWorld 100, 2009, and 2010 InformationWeek 500, and the 2011 InfoWorld Green 15 Award.

Colisto holds a B.B.A in management information systems and an M.S. in information systems from Pace University.

He lives with his wife and two children in Marlboro, New Jersey.

James H. Comfort

Jim Comfort received his Ph.D. from the Massachusetts Institute of Technology in 1988. He joined IBM Research in 1988 and worked across the boundaries from Research to Systems and Technology Group on new product introduction in a variety of development and product management roles. Jim held a number of executive positions within IBM Systems Group, spanning technology development, systems development, and product line management, as well as roles in IBM Corporate Strategy. For the past two years, he was part of the Enterprise Initiatives team in Corporate Strategy, defining IBM's cloud computing strategy from technology, offerings, and business model perspectives. He is currently vice president, Integrated Delivery Platforms, Cloud Computing. He is responsible for technical and investment strategy to accelerate and expand asset utilization in IBM's outsourcing business, defining roadmaps that consistently deliver innovations such as cloud computing capabilities to IBM's outsourcing innovation.

Barbra Cooper is group VP and CIO for Toyota Motor Sales (TMS) North America., Inc. She is responsible for the strategy, development, and operation of all systems and technology that support TMS.

Barbra Cooper

With a career spanning more than 30 years in IT, Barbra joined Toyota in 1996 as VP of IS. Previously, she held the position of group VP and CIO for MicroAge Corp., CIO for Maricopa County in Phoenix, VP of Technology for American Express, and director of IS for Miller & Paine.

Barbra was named one of the Top 100 Women in Computing in 1996, a national honor recognizing women in the IS field who have achieved both technical expertise and advanced management positions. Additionally, she was honored as one of *Computerworld*'s Premier IT Leaders in 2001. Cooper received the *CIO* 100 Award in 2005. *CIO Insight* magazine ranked her sixth of the top 100 global CIOs in 2007, and *CIO* magazine's Executive Council awarded her the 2007 Distinguished Member Award for Most Valuable Content. She has also been recognized for her automotive industry achievements, including the 2000, 2005, and 2007 *Automotive News* awards for the 100 Leading Women in the automotive industry. Barbra was inducted into the *CIO* Hall of Fame in 2007 for strongly influencing the evolution of this young profession over the last decade and for expanding IT strategic possibilities.

Tim Crawford is VP of information technology and CIO of All Covered, a division of Konica Minolta Business Solutions USA Inc.

He has over 20 years of information technology experience in operations, infrastructure, information security, and core applications. Areas of focus include cloud computing, infrastructure optimization, and key game-changing strategies for IT organizations.

Tim Crawford
Photographer: Gene Gouss, Gene Gouss Photography. Title: Tim Crawford, All Covered/Konica Minolta. Copyright date: 5/13/11

Tim regularly speaks at industry conferences and has written for leading publications. Tim serves on a number of boards, including the Society for Information Management (SIM) and Data Center Pulse.

Tim received an MBA in international business with honors and a bachelor of science degree in computer information systems, both from Golden Gate University.

Martin Davis is the EVP, technology and operations group of Wells Fargo & Company. He provides executive leadership to the Technology Integration Office and is accountable for overseeing technology integration efforts for Wells Fargo, ensuring the highest level of security for customer data,

Martin Davis

continuing the availability of systems, and minimizing transition risk for the enterprise.

Prior to Wachovia's acquisition by Wells Fargo, Martin was Wachovia's corporate CIO, where he led more than 2,700 employees and oversaw Wachovia's application development and maintenance activities. Martin was accountable for the strategic and business processes within the CIO organization and was responsible for the consistency, standardization, and prioritization of all centrally driven technology initiatives across the enterprise. Martin began his career with Wachovia in 1985 and served in a number of roles supporting technology functions for Wachovia's Commercial, Wealth, and Brokerage groups.

He received his bachelor of arts degree in business administration from Winston-Salem State University in North Carolina and is a graduate of the Young Executives Institute and the Executive Leadership Program at the University of North Carolina–Chapel Hill. He has been recognized as one of the 50 Most Important African Americans in Technology by *US Black Engineer* magazine and as one of the 75 Most Powerful African Americans in Corporate America by *Black Enterprise* magazine.

Stephen Gold

Stephen J. Gold is the senior vice president and chief information officer of Avaya. He is responsible for all aspects of Avaya's technology strategy, as well as leading IT excellence across Avaya business operations and systems globally. This includes identifying and prioritizing strategic IT initiatives to ensure Avaya remains at the forefront of technology while driving efficiencies across business functions.

Prior to joining Avaya, Stephen was executive vice president, CIO, and corporate chief technology officer of GSI Commerce. He also served as senior vice president and CIO for Medco Health Solutions, and he has held other positions of increasing responsibility at Medco, Dun & Bradstreet, and Sandoz Pharmaceuticals.

Stephen holds a BS in computer science from St. John's University.

Leslie L. Gordon

In January 2009, **Leslie Gordon** was named vice president, application and infrastructure services management, reporting to the IBM CIO. The mission of her global organization is to deliver world-class IT services and enable IBM's internal transformation by leveraging IT to support IBM's enterprise strategy.

In prior roles, she has been an executive in the Storage and Technology organization, responsible for leading growth initiatives to leverage the power of optimization and virtualization across the infrastructure layer. The Enterprise Computing Model project was launched in 3Q 2007 to address current client priorities (enhance "green" corporate standing, reduce IT infrastructure costs, optimization, virtualization, power and cooling constraints) as well as an opportunity for IBM to collaborate more effectively across the entire depth and breadth of technology, financial, and business solutions for clients. This transformational project encompassed significant implementation within the IBM Global Account, the Strategic Outsourcing (services) client base, and continuing development of solutions for the external client marketplace.

Leslie has held multiple leadership and management roles in hardware and software product development primarily in the IBM printer and copier business areas and later in the IBM Publishing Systems Business Unit headquartered in Boulder, Colorado. In addition, Leslie has extensive experience in a wide range of services-related management roles in the Americas as well as an international assignment to Sydney, Australia. These include project executive roles at two large outsourcing contracts in the banking and aerospace industries, and senior delivery project executive and delivery management. She is also a certified project manager.

Leslie graduated with a bachelor of science degree in mechanical engineering from Duke University. She joined IBM in 1982 as a manufacturing engineer in Charlotte, North Carolina, and has had extensive experience across multiple business areas and divisions of IBM.

Allan Hackney

Allan Hackney is SVP and chief information officer at John Hancock Financial Services with oversight of the company's Wealth Management and Insurance technical teams. In this role, Allan is accountable for developing and executing strategies that increase productivity and efficiency, improve operating risk management, and enhance the technical talent across the entire enterprise. Allan joined John Hancock from AIG Consumer Finance Group where, as CIO, he championed the effort to reposition autonomous banking and lending operations into a more integrated global expansion platform to enable significant expansion.

Allan graduated with a bachelor's degree from Colgate University. He is a Faculty Fellow at The Levin Institute, the State University of New York's international graduate business school in New York City. Allan is also on the regional board of BuildOn, a nonprofit organization that empowers youth in the United States to make a positive difference in their communities while helping people of developing countries increase their self-reliance through education.

Kim Hammonds

Kim Hammonds is chief information officer of The Boeing Company. Hammonds is responsible for the IT strategy, operations, processes, and more than 8,500 IT people of the world's largest aerospace company. She has responsibility for supporting the growth of Boeing's business by partnering with the business units on IT-related revenue-generating programs and oversees all aspects of information security across the global reach of the company.

Prior to joining Boeing, she was director of Americas Manufacturing Operations at Dell, where she was responsible for global systems development for service logistics, supply chain, and quality systems. She was also responsible for IT production support for all 18 global manufacturing operations.

Kim received an MBA from Western Michigan University and a bachelor's degree in mechanical engineering from the University of Michigan.

Tyson Hartman

As Avanade's chief technology officer, **Tyson Hartman** is responsible for Avanade's technology vision, solutions, and R&D investments. Focusing on how best to leverage the latest Microsoft technology to solve customer problems, Tyson leads the incubation and engineering teams to deliver differentiated solutions across the complete enterprise IT life cycle.

Tyson joined Avanade in June 2000 and has held various positions in his more than ten years with the company. Prior to his role as Global CTO, he served as Americas CTO, leading teams on major technology, strategy, and quality initiatives. As a member of Avanade's first engineering group, he was instrumental in developing solutions and assets for some of Avanade's first key customers. Previously, Tyson was with Accenture, where he focused on e-commerce and high-volume online transaction processing systems in the high-tech, communications, and consumer products industries.

Tyson is a sought-after expert and author, with particular expertise in subjects such as cloud computing, SOA, application

Donagh Herlihy

integration, and high-volume transaction systems. Tyson holds a bachelor's degree in computer science and computer engineering from the University of Southern California.

Donagh Herlihy is SVP and CIO at Avon Products, Inc. He leads an IT organization of 1,500 professionals and is responsible for global IT strategy and operations. His team provides the business systems and technology infrastructure supporting Avon's business operations in more than 60 countries and is responsible for enabling online business for more than six million Avon representatives worldwide. Major initiatives include driving growth through Web and mobile platforms for Avon representatives and consumers and driving efficiency through global ERP.

Prior to joining Avon in 2008, he drove the organizational and business process transformation at the Wrigley Company as CIO, VP of human resources, and VP of supply chain strategy and planning. Herlihy also spent six years at Gillette, leading IT at its Duracell subsidiary. Earlier in his career, while based in the UK, he worked in manufacturing, business process reengineering, and IT in the consumer goods and automotive sectors.

Donagh holds a BS in industrial engineering from the Dublin Institute of Technology and Trinity College, Dublin, Ireland, and has completed the Executive Program at the University of Michigan, Ross School of Business. He is a board member of the American Red Cross in Westchester, New York.

John F. Hill is Global CIO of Veyance Technologies, the exclusive manufacturer of Goodyear Engineered Products worldwide. He was a former chief technology officer at Siemens IT Solutions and Services, where he was responsible for all technology aspects of the firm's IT services clients

John Hill

and the 4,700 Siemens IT Solutions and Services employees in North America. Throughout his career, John has consistently demonstrated innovative approaches to IT strategies that drive business competitiveness.

Prior to joining Siemens, he was vice president and CIO at Praxair, Inc., the largest supplier of industrial gases in North and South America, with $6 billion in revenue and 24,500 employees. Prior to Praxair, he was vice president of IT at the Perkin-Elmer Corporation, leading a global team of IT professionals serving employees in 14 countries. John has also run a successful independent IT consultancy. His early IT experiences include positions with Combustion Engineering, Pitney Bowes, and Andersen Consulting. He has also served on the board of directors for numerous technology firms.

John received a BA from Princeton University where he majored in politics and minored in mathematics.

Mark Hillman

Mark Hillman leads strategy and implementation teams for Compuware products and services. Mark ensures Compuware's extensive portfolio continues solving operational challenges as applications and infrastructure increase in complexity. He collaborates with customers, analysts, and industry thought leaders to identify the most pressing IT challenges businesses face today in order to ensure the strategy and implementation of Compuware products and services provide superior value.

Prior to Compuware Corporation, Mark held senior IT executive positions at General Motors, including director of GM Global Computing Operations and director of Supply Chain Operations. Before General Motors, Mark served in marketing, product management, and information technology at Texas Instruments.

Randy Krotowski

During his 21 years with Chevron, **Randy Krotowski** has held a variety of technology and business management positions. As manager, Strategic Planning for Chevron's IT division, he led a $270 million effort to upgrade Chevron's global infrastructure and Web application development capabilities. He has held management positions in organizational development, marketing, engineering, joint ventures, Total Quality Management, and large capital project management.

Randy holds a bachelor's degree in chemical engineering from the University of Toronto and a master's in business administration from Golden Gate University. He is active in a number of engineering, IT, and project management associations. He chairs the Technology Strategy and Transformation Standing Committee.

Tony Leng

Tony Leng is a managing director of Diversified Search and heads the CIO, Technology, and Private Equity practices. He also leads the firm's San Francisco office. Previously, Tony was Managing Partner of Hodge Partners.

His clients include public and private companies where he has placed board members and C-level executives. He has conducted senior management assignments for Hypercom, JDA Software, MSquared, QRS, Broadvision, Delta Dental, Catholic Healthcare West, Kaiser Permanente, Visa, Symmetricom, Key Principal Partners, OpenTV, Cerberus Capital, The Riverside Company, Vistage, and the Young Presidents' Organization.

Prior to his executive search experience, Tony was a board member of three public companies and CEO of a $600 million public diversified IT company that controlled businesses in software, communications, services, distribution, integration, defense technology, and outsourcing. Before that, Tony ran a more than $1 billion division of a telephone company focused on corporate users and had responsibility for all data services and networking products. While at the telephone company, he was founder and chairman of its ISP and a board member of its two million–subscriber cell phone–associated company. Previously, Tony was the CEO of a multibranch, 600-person credit bureau that provided consumer and commercial information. During his five-year tenure, he grew the enterprise value fivefold.

Tony uses his operating and board experience, combined with the knowledge that he has gained in the search industry, to drill down and understand at a nuanced level what his clients are seeking to achieve as they build their teams and boards. His experience in working at both large and small companies has made him particularly effective in understanding the challenges and leadership requirements that businesses face as they grow.

Tony received a bachelor of commerce (with honors) from the University of Cape Town, South Africa. He is qualified as a chartered accountant and certified public accountant.

Tod Nielsen joined VMware in January 2009 as chief operating officer. Prior to VMware, he served as president and chief executive officer of Borland Software since November 2005. Prior to Borland, he held several key executive management positions at leading software companies including Microsoft, BEA, and Oracle. Tod brings more than 20 years of leadership experience in enterprise software and application development to VMware. Prior to Borland, he served as senior vice president, marketing and global sales support for Oracle Corporation.

Tod Nielsen

Prior to Oracle, he was the chief marketing officer and executive vice president of engineering at BEA Systems, where he had overall responsibility for BEA's worldwide marketing strategy and operations, as well as all research and development operations. Tod joined BEA after the acquisition of his private company, Crossgain Inc., where he served as its chief executive officer. Tod also spent twelve years with Microsoft Corporation in various roles, including general manager of Database and Developer Tools, vice president of Developer Tools, and vice president of Microsoft's Platform Group.

Bertrand Odinet has served as vice president and chief information officer of Freeport McMoRan Copper & Gold since 2003. Since joining Freeport-McMoRan Copper and Gold in 1995, Bert has assumed responsibilities in corporate IT, operational improvement, merger integration, and financial shared services. Prior to joining FCX, Bert held several management positions with Arthur Andersen and Andersen Consulting, where he was a management consultant in the manufacturing, aerospace and defense, and oil and gas industries. He received his B.S. in civil engineering from Louisiana State University.

Bertrand Odinet

Tom Peck is the chief information officer (CIO) of Levi Strauss & Co., responsible for leading the company's global information technology operations and services. Tom reports to Chief Executive Officer John Anderson and is a member of the company's worldwide leadership team.

Tom Peck

Tom has a history of creating technology solutions for global consumer and entertainment brands via large-scale investments in SAP and Oracle, vendor-managed inventory (VMI) and customer relationship management. Prior to joining Levi Strauss & Co., he was the CIO of MGM Mirage, supporting 70,000 employees across 17 global resorts such as the Bellagio and MGM Grand. As CIO, he led numerous innovations across hotel and casino operations as well as the company's 800+ retail and restaurant venues.

Before joining MGM Mirage, Tom held numerous roles within General Electric Company, including CIO of NBC Universal's global entertainment businesses, which included television, motion pictures, home entertainment, consumer products, and theme parks and resorts. While CIO, his team implemented a global enterprise-wide project that spanned 15 operating companies in 28 countries via SAP and other systems platforms, upgraded 25-year-old legacy systems, simplified numerous processes, and expanded VMI to more than 50 retail partners around the world.

Tom began his career in the United States Marine Corps holding numerous finance and technology jobs. He is also a certified Six Sigma Master Black Belt and is proficient in process optimization strategies such as lean supply chain. Tom earned his bachelor's degree from the United States Naval Academy with distinction in economics, and a master's degree in management from the Naval Postgraduate School.

Steve Phillips is senior vice president and chief information officer for Avnet, Inc. He is also a member of the Avnet executive board and a corporate officer.

Steve Phillips

In 2011, *Computerworld* named Steve a Premier 100 IT Leader. This lifetime recognition honors executives for exceptional technology leadership, innovative ideas to address business challenges, and effectively managing IT strategies.

Steve holds a BSc (Hons) in electronic engineering from Essex University and a postgraduate diploma in management studies from Thames Valley University. He is a Fellow of the Institution of Engineering & Technology.

Steve Phillpott is CIO for Amylin Pharmaceuticals, a leading provider of drugs for the treatment of diabetes. Mr. Phillpott has over 20 years of broad experience in information technology and management that includes Fortune 500 and large global manufacturing companies.

Steve Phillpott

Prior to joining Amylin, Steve was CIO of Proflowers.com, a high-volume e-commerce retailer. Steve was VP of IT for Global Enterprise Applications at Invitrogen (now Life Technologies Corp). Prior to that, he held various leadership positions at companies, including Memec (Avnet), Gateway, and Qualcomm.

Steve received his BS in engineering from the U.S. Naval Academy and has his MBA in technology management.

Mark Polansky is a senior client partner and the managing director of Korn/Ferry International's Information Technology Center of Expertise for North America. With more than 25 years of executive search experience, all in technology, Mark has extensively recruited chief information officers, chief technology officers, and

Mark Polansky

other senior IT leaders across a wide range of vertical industry sectors. He also has expertise in recruiting for both general and technical management for public and private high-tech companies, managed service providers, professional services organizations, venture firms, and their portfolio companies.

Before entering the search field, Mark spent 11 years in computer programming, systems management, and business development at two large information technology organizations engaged in the development, support, and marketing of information systems in the financial services and higher education sectors.

Mark previously taught computer science at Pratt Institute, Brooklyn College, and Southern Connecticut State University. He currently serves on the advisory board of Columbia University's executive graduate program in information technology management.

He frequently addresses conferences and writes on information systems subjects as well as career management and human resources topics, and he is the creator of the "Executive Career Counsel" column in *CIO Magazine*. He is a member of the Society for Information Management, previously serving as chairman and president of the New York Metro Chapter. Mark currently serves on the advisory boards of The Information Technology Senior Management Forum, the national organization dedicated to fostering executive talent among African-American IT professionals; and HITEC, the Hispanic Information Technology Executive Council.

Mark holds a master's degree in computer science from Pratt Institute and a bachelor's degree in mathematics and electrical engineering from Union College.

Tony Scott

Tony Scott joined Microsoft Corp. in February 2008 as corporate vice president and chief information officer (CIO). Under Scott's leadership, Microsoft IT is responsible for security, infrastructure, messaging, and business applications for all of Microsoft, including support of the product groups, the corporate business groups, and the global sales and marketing organization.

Before joining Microsoft, Tony was the senior vice president and chief information officer for Walt Disney Co., where he led planning, implementation and operations of Disney IT systems and infrastructure across the company. He also held the position of CTO, Information Systems and Services, at General Motors Corp. (GM), where he was responsible for defining the information technology computing and telecommunications strategy, architecture, and standards across all of GM's businesses globally.

Tony has a bachelor of science in information systems management from the University of San Francisco and also holds a Juris Doctorate with a concentration in intellectual property and international law from Santa Clara University.

Esat Sezer was named senior vice president and chief information officer on October 11, 2006, at Coca-Cola Enterprises. He oversees the company's technology and information capabilities and reports to John F. Brock, president and chief executive officer. Esat has more than 25 years of global IT experience. Most recently, he served as corporation vice president and chief information officer for Whirlpool Corporation, a position he held since 2002.

Esat Sezer

Prior to joining Whirlpool Corporation as vice president, Global Information Services in 2001, he held several positions of increasing responsibility with Colgate-Palmolive Co., including director, Global Information Technology (1999–2001); director, Europe/Africa/Middle East Division (1996–1998); associate director, Global Applications (1996–1997); and director, Information Technology (1994–1996 in Warsaw, Poland; 1991–1994 in Istanbul, Turkey). From 1988 to 1991, he was a senior consultant at Andersen Consulting in London.

Born and raised in Istanbul, he received his bachelor of science degree in electrical engineering from Istanbul Technical University. Esat is currently a board member on the advisory group for the nonprofit organization Computers for Youth and an advisory board member of several technology companies.

David Smoley is the senior vice president and chief information officer of Flextronics International, a $26 billion global manufacturing and services provider operating in

Dave Smoley

more than 30 countries worldwide. *Information Week* recently ranked Dave as one of the top 50 global CIOs, calling him an IT leader changing the business world.

Prior to his time at Flextronics, Dave served as vice president and chief information officer at Honeywell's Aerospace Electronics Systems. Dave's extensive IT career also includes management positions with General Electric, where he most recently held the position of director and chief information officer for GE Power Controls in Barcelona, Spain.

Dave has a BA in computer science from Clemson University and an MBA from the University of Virginia's Darden School of Business.

Randy Spratt

Randall (Randy) N. Spratt is executive vice president, chief technology officer, and chief information officer for McKesson Corporation.

As CTO, Randy guides the overall technology direction for the company's health care technology products and provides support and guidance for application development processes company-wide.

As CIO, Randy is responsible for all technology initiatives within the corporation. He has been with McKesson for more than 18 years, most recently as chief process officer for McKesson Provider Technologies (MPT), the company's medical software and services division based in Alpharetta,

Georgia. He also managed MPT's Business Development, Information Technology, and Strategic Planning offices, as well as MPT's Technology Services business.

Prior to joining McKesson, Randy held executive positions of increasing responsibility at the start-up Advanced Laboratory Systems (ALS), culminating with the role of chief operations officer. ALS was acquired by HBOC in 1996, which in turn was acquired by McKesson in 1999, and Randy took on responsibility for HBOC's laboratory systems business shortly thereafter. Following the acquisition of HBOC by McKesson in 1999, Randy relocated to Georgia to become part of the reconstructed management team.

Randy earned a bachelor of science degree in biology, with a minor in computer science, from the University of Utah.

Lauren C. States

As vice president, CTO for Cloud Computing and Growth Initiatives on the IBM Corporate Strategy team, **Lauren States** is responsible for the technology strategy for IBM's growth initiatives, including cloud computing, Smarter Planet, business analytics, and emerging markets.

In her previous role as vice president of Cloud Computing for IBM Software Group, Lauren led a global team responsible for establishing market leadership for cloud computing. Her team engaged directly with clients to deliver leading-edge capabilities, incorporating their technology requirements into IBM's strategy, offerings, and plans.

As a senior executive on IBM's Integration and Values Team, Lauren played a leadership role in a company-wide initiative called the Client Value Initiative—a strategic reshaping of IBM's value creation. She was responsible for integrating and transforming IBM's processes for skills development, knowledge management, and career progression for IBM's professional sales force.

In a previous role, Lauren led worldwide Technical Sales and Sales Enablement for IBM Software Group. She was responsible for the 5,000+ technical sales organization and for sales enablement and customer software deployment across IBM's total software business.

Lauren joined IBM in 1978 as a systems engineer in New York City and has held a variety of leadership positions since that time. In 1991, Lauren joined IBM's client/server business initiative, taking responsibility for developing new markets and laying the groundwork for distributed computing. Later, she led IBM's Midwest sales territory, delivering e-business and early Web solutions to all types of clients.

Lauren graduated from the University of Pennsylvania Wharton School with a bachelor of science degree. She has served on the IBM Technical Leadership Team, which is responsible for the development and advancement of IBM's technical workforce. As a role model and mentor to women and minorities around the world, Lauren co-chairs the IBM North America Black Constituency Council. She is chair of the board of visitors for the Northeastern University College of Business and serves on the International House, New York, board of trustees. She also serves on the board of directors for MoJo (www.momsandjobs.com) and is a member of the Executive Leadership Council.

In 2003, Lauren received the Women of Color Technology Conference's Managerial Excellence Award from Career Communications Group, Inc. In 2006, she was recognized as one of the 25 Most Influential Black Women in American Business by *The Network Journal*. She was also named one of the Top 100 Blacks in Technology in 2006 and 2007 by Career Communications Group, Inc.

Pat Toole

Pat Toole is general manager of Maintenance and Technical Support Services—Global Technology Services at IBM. Previously, he served as IBM's chief information officer. As CIO, he was responsible for advancing the company's transformational agenda and aligning information technology investments to the business strategy. Prior to that, Pat was general manager of Intellectual Property at IBM, overseeing the direction of the company's intellectual property portfolio and global patent program.

Pat joined IBM in 1984 and has held a variety of executive and management positions across the company, including vice president of Enterprise On Demand Transformation and Information Technology and general manager of Engineering and Technology Services. Pat holds a bachelor of science in electrical engineering from the University of Notre Dame and a master of business administration from Queens University of Charlotte.

Clif Triplett

Clifton (Clif) Triplett was named vice president and CIO of Baker in 2008. He joined the company from Motorola, where he served as VP and CIO of the Network and Enterprise Group, and most recently as VP, Global Services. Prior to that, he held a variety of IT leadership roles with General Motors, Allied Signal, and Entergy Services.

He holds a degree in engineering from the U.S. Military Academy and a master's degree in computer information systems from Boston University. Clif is also a member of the executive board for the School of Engineering at Southern Methodist University and is a member of *ComputerWorld*'s Premier 100 IT Leaders for 2010.

Joe Weinman
Bob Rannells
photography

Joe Weinman leads a global team focused on strategy and industry solutions for the communications, media, and entertainment verticals in HP's Worldwide Industry Solutions organization. He is a longtime veteran of the industry, having held positions of increasing responsibility at the world's largest telecommunications company, and he is a frequent keynoter, a prolific inventor, and an author/blogger. Joe is a well-known cloud computing evangelist, creating "Cloudonomics" at the intersection of cloud computing, ROI/business value, and economics.

RECOMMENDED READING

Barlow, Mike, and Michael Minelli. *Partnering with the CIO: The Future of IT Sales Seen Through the Eyes of Key Decision Makers.* Hoboken, NJ: John Wiley & Sons, 2008.

Barlow, Mike, and David B. Thomas. *The Executive's Guide to Enterprise Social Media Strategy: How Social Networks Are Radically Transforming Your Business.* Hoboken, NJ: John Wiley & Sons, 2011.

Benioff, Marc. *Behind the Cloud: The Untold Story of How Salesforce.com Went from Idea to Billion-dollar Company and Revolutionized an Industry.* San Francisco: Jossey-Bass, 2009.

Broadbent, Marianne, and Ellen S. Kitzis. *The New CIO Leader: Setting the Agenda and Delivering Results.* Boston: Harvard Business School Press, 2005.

Collins, Jim. *Good to Great: Why Some Companies Make the Leap . . . and Others Don't.* New York: HarperBusiness, 2001.

Covey, Stephen R. *The 7 Habits of Highly Effective People: Powerful Lessons in Personal Change.* New York: Free Press, 1989, 2004.

Deming, W. Edwards. *The New Economy for Industry, Government, Education.* Cambridge, MA: MIT Center for Advanced Educational Services, 1994.

Eiras, José Carlos. *The Practical CIO: A Common Sense Guide for Successful IT Leadership.* Hoboken, NJ: John Wiley & Sons, 2010.

Friedman, Thomas L. *The World Is Flat: A Brief History of the 21st Century.* New York: Picador/Farrar, Straus and Giroux, 2005.

Greenleaf, Robert K. *Servant Leadership: A Journey into the Nature of Legitimate Power & Greatness.* New York: Paulist Press, 2002.

Hammer, Michael. *Beyond Reengineering: How the Process-Centered Organization Is Changing Our Work and Our Lives.* New York: HarperBusiness, 1996.

High, Peter A. *World Class IT: Why Businesses Succeed When IT Triumphs.* San Francisco: Jossey-Bass, 2009.

Juran, J. M. *Juran on Quality by Design: The New Steps for Planning Quality into Goods and Services.* New York: Free Press, 1992.

Katzenbach, Jon R., and Douglas K. Smith. *The Wisdom of Teams: Creating the High-Performance Organization.* Boston: Harvard Business School Press, 1993.

Kidder, Tracy. *The Soul of a New Machine.* New York: Little, Brown and Company, 1981.

Kiechel, Walter. *The Lords of Strategy: The Secret Intellectual History of the New Corporate World.* Boston: Harvard Business School Press, 2010.

Kim, W. Chan, and Renee Mauborgne. *Blue Ocean Strategy: How to Create Uncontested Market Space and Make the Competition Irrelevant.* Boston: Harvard Business School Press, 2005.

Kotter, John P. *John P. Kotter on What Leaders Really Do.* Boston: Harvard Business School Press, 1999.

Krishnan, M. S., and C. K. Prahalad. *The New Age of Innovation: Driving Co-Created Value Through Global Networks.* New York: McGraw Hill, 2008.

Li, Charlene. *Open Leadership: How Social Technology Can Transform the Way You Lead.* San Francisco: Jossey-Bass, 2010.

Linthicum, David S. *Cloud Computing and SOA Convergence in Your Enterprise: A Step-by-Step Guide.* New York: Addison-Wesley Professional, 2009.

Lutchen, Mark D. *Managing IT as a Business: A Survival Guide for CEOs.* Hoboken, New Jersey: John Wiley & Sons, 2004.

May, Matthew E. *The Elegant Solution: Toyota's Formula for Master Innovation.* New York: Free Press, 2007.

Mirchandani, Vinnie. *The New Polymath: Profiles in Compound-Technology Innovations.* Hoboken, NJ: John Wiley & Sons, 2010.

Muller, Hunter. *The Transformational CIO: Leadership and Innovation Strategies for IT Executives in a Rapidly Changing World.* Hoboken, New Jersey: John Wiley & Sons, 2011.

Rosenberg, Scott. *Dreaming in Code.* New York: Crown Publishers, 2007.

Smith, Gregory S. *Straight to the Top: Becoming a World-Class CIO.* Hoboken, NJ: John Wiley & Sons, 2006.

Trowbridge, Ben. *Cloud Sourcing the Corporation: Strategies You Can Use, 100 Vendors You Should Know.* Dallas: Alsbridge, 2011.

Tugend, Alina. *Better by Mistake: The Unexpected Benefits of Being Wrong.* New York: Riverhead Books, 2011.

Watkins, Michael. *The First 90 Days: Critical Strategies for New Leaders at All Levels.* Boston: Harvard Business School Press, 2003.

Zweifel, Thomas D. *Culture Clash: Managing the Global High-Performance Team.* New York: Select Books, 2003.

ABOUT THE AUTHOR

Hunter Muller is president and CEO of HMG Strategy LLC, a global IT strategy consulting firm based in Westport, Connecticut. Mr. Muller has nearly three decades of experience in business strategy consulting. His primary focus is IT organization development, leadership, and business alignment. His concepts and programs have been used successfully by premier corporations worldwide to improve executive performance, enhance collaboration, elevate the role of IT, and align enterprise strategy across the topmost levels of management. He lives in Fairfield, Connecticut, with his wife and their two children. For additional information, please contact Hunter directly via e-mail at hunterm@hmgstrategy.com.

ABOUT HMG STRATEGY LLC

HMG Strategy LLC is the fastest-growing thought leadership organization dedicated to empowering chief information officers with leadership, management, and technology support and advice through an extensive network of the world's most successful IT leaders.

The firm's unique CIO Executive Leadership Series offers unique event experiences to build relationships with peers and gain the latest insights and best practices for driving increased business value through the use of information technology.

HMG Strategy events enable IT leaders to leverage the power of an extensive network of more than 10,000 highly talented CIOs and senior executives from multiple sectors of the global economy. These events raise thought leadership, knowledge sharing, and networking to the highest levels.

Additionally, the firm's partnership with the world's leading executive search firms provides IT leaders with invaluable insights and opportunities for career advancement. For additional information, please visit www.hmgstrategy.com or send an e-mail to hunterm@hmgstrategy.com.

INDEX